FINGERS TELL THE STORY

Fingerplays, Pantomimes, and Litanies for the Very Young

Compiled by Debbie Stroh

Edited by the Board for Parish Services Staff
Editor: Jane L. Fryar

Publishing House
St. Louis

Editorial Assistant: Beverly Bangert
Editorial Secretary: Carla Haeberle

Copyright © 1989 by Concordia Publishing House, 3558 South Jefferson Avenue, St. Louis, MO 63118-3968. Manufactured in the United States of America.

All rights reserved. No part of this publication may be reproduced, stored in a retrieval system, or transmitted, in any form or by any means, electronic, mechanical, photocopying, recording, or otherwise, without the prior written permission of Concordia Publishing House.

This publication is also available in braille and in sightsaving print for the visually impaired. Write to Library for the Blind, 1333 South Kirkwood Road, St. Louis, MO 63122-7295. Allow at least one month for processing.

Special thanks to Alison Atwood, Lesley Beck, Elizabeth Becker, Chris Belk, Heather Belk, Jennifer Boston, Katie Deelo, Lindsay Dunlap, Cori Freudenberg, Sara Freudenberg, Daniel Lee, Brian Marsh, Jill Marsh, Kristin Marsh, Tony Moeller, Julia Moskoff, Michael Schmidt, and Samantha Schwab for their contribution of creative artwork to *Fingers Tell the Story*.

Contents

Foreword	5
"Baby Jesus Is Born!" Finger Plays	7
"God Made Me" Finger Plays	15
"I'm Growing" Finger Plays	18
"God's Love" Finger Plays	21
"When Jesus Died and Rose Again" Finger Plays	30
"The World God Made" Finger Plays	33
"My Family" Finger Plays	41
"God's Book" Finger Plays	43
"God's House" Finger Plays	44
"Friends" Finger Plays	47
"I Can Help" Finger Plays	48
Old Testament Bible Story Pantomimes	50
New Testament Bible Story Pantomimes	56
"Thank You, God" Litanies	75
"Help Us, God" Litanies	79
"I'm Sorry" Litanies	83
"All about Jesus" Litanies	84
"Praise God" Litanies	87
Contributors	90
Topical Index	91
Index of First Lines	93

Foreword

Fingers Tell the Story: Finger Plays, Pantomimes, and Litanies for the Very Young will help teachers and parents lead young children in simple activities designed to reinforce Scriptural truths in a way that is enjoyable and educationally sound.

Most of the activities in this book originally appeared in Sunday school, vacation Bible school, and Christian day school curricula published by Concordia Publishing House. Some activities are familiar and beloved by teachers and pupils throughout our church; others are relatively new and fresh. We have tried to choose those activities that have proven most helpful to teachers and most fun for children. The activities have been selected primarily for children three to five years old. They can be used in a variety of Christian early childhood programs. Most are also appropriate for home use.

Notes to Leaders

In general, children enjoy finger plays, rhymes, prayers, and pantomimes in which they can participate. Here are some hints for keeping young children interested and involved:

1. As you choose and lead activities, keep the children's abilities in mind. Don't expect too much too soon. Some activities in this book are best kept until the children are a bit older.
2. Children learn best when they are active. Encourage the children to add their own motions if an activity doesn't already suggest them.
3. Don't use complicated motions in any activity. Simplify the ones given in this book if they seem too difficult for your children.
4. Speak and act reverently, especially as you lead the children in litanies or responsive prayers. Expect the pupils to imitate both your attitudes and your actions.
5. As you lead the children in Bible story echo pantomimes, remember to keep both words and actions short and simple because the children will "echo" these after you. Stress the *words* of the activity. Choose only the very simplest echo pantomimes for use with three-year-olds.
6. Don't insist that all the children participate in the actions. Rather, keep your focus on the *words* of the activity.
7. Remember that young children enjoy repetition. Don't be reluctant to repeat a particular selection several times in a row during a class period. And feel free to use the children's favorite selections often throughout the year.

"Baby Jesus Is Born!" Finger Plays

Mary and the Angel

Mary saw an angel.
Look up.
First she was afraid.
Place arm over eyes.
Then she listened carefully.
Cup hand behind ear.
This is what he said:
Touch lips.

"You will have a baby,
Pretend to rock baby in arms.
Jesus, God's own son.
Point to heaven.
He will be the Savior,
Bow head.
Sent for everyone."
With sweeping motion of hand, indicate classmates.

Mary then was happy.
Smile and clap hands.
Are you happy, too?
Point to classmates.
God, you see, sent Jesus
Point to heaven.
Down to earth.
Move finger downward.
For you.
Point to classmates.

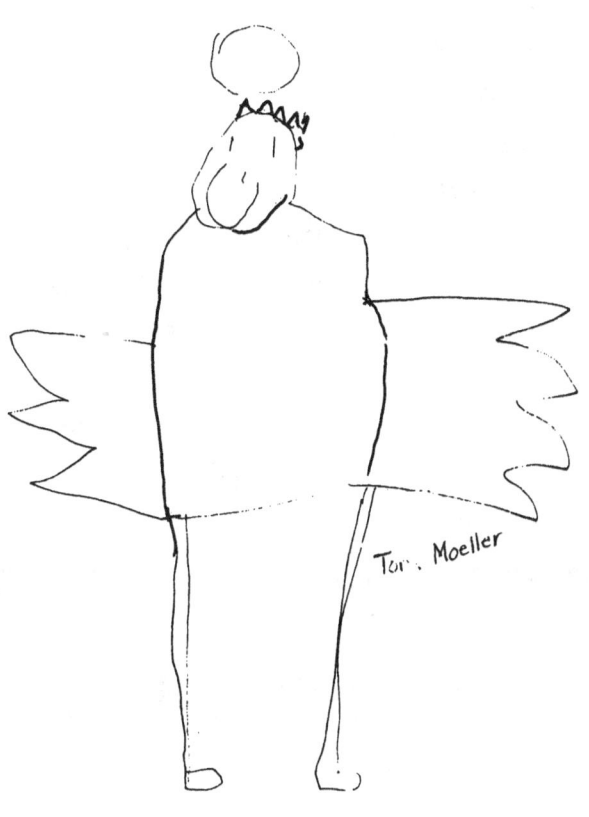

The Best Present of All

Christmas presents remind me
Form fingers into shape of a box.
That animals gave Jesus their manger,
Cross arms in X-shape of manger legs.
And Mary gave Jesus her love,
Hug self.
And shepherds gave Jesus their praises,
Fold hands.
And Wise Men gave Jesus their gold;
Rub fingers together as if feeling money.
But most of all, Christmas presents remind me
Form fingers into shape of a box.
That the Father in heaven gave us Jesus,
Cradle and rock arms.
The best present of all!
Hands outstretched, palms up.

One Night in Bethlehem

One night in Bethlehem ...
Sheep ate grass.
Pretend to chew.
Shepherds watched.
Shade eyes with hand.
Angels sang.
Cup hands around mouth.
Jesus slept.
Rest heads on hands.
Shepherds prayed.
Kneel and fold hands.
Mary loved.
Put hand over heart.
Joseph helped.

Kristin Marsh

Come, Lord Jesus!

Come, Lord Jesus,
Extend right hand in gesture of greeting.
Come with love.
Hands flat on chest, over heart.
Come, our Savior from above.
Both hands extended out and up, in welcome.

Please forgive us
Arms folded, head bowed.
When we're bad.
Make sign of cross.
Live in us and make us glad.
Smile, frame face with hands.

Wise Men

Let's play we are Wise Men.
On camels we jump.
Jump, landing with legs apart.
We ride to see Jesus.
Bump, bumpity, bump.
Holding "reins," jog body up and down at knees.
We ride over mountains.
We ride night and day.
Continue riding motion.
God's star in the heavens
Take one hand off "reins," and point to "star" overhead.
Will show us the way.
Point to "road" ahead.
Jump down from camels.
Jump, landing with legs together.
And bring in your gifts.
Walk in place, carrying "gifts."
Give them to Jesus.
Lay "gifts" on floor.

Walk to the Manger

We go to see Jesus;
God sent Him, you know,
   Point upward.
God's very own Son,
He loves us all so!
   Hug self.

We play we are shepherds
And walk with a stick.
   Pretend to lean on crook.
We walk to the manger
Quicker than quick.
   Walk in place.

Happy, Happy, Happy

Happy, happy, happy,
   Point to your smiling faces.
As we wait today
   Point to heaven.
For the baby Jesus
   Cradle a baby in your arms.
Sleeping on the hay.
   Hug yourself.

Happy, happy, happy,
   Point to your smiling faces.
Jesus, God's own Son
   Point to yourself.
Born on Christmas morning
   Cradle a baby in your arms.
Loves us everyone!
   Rest head on hands, close eyes.

Happy, happy, happy,
   Point to your smiling faces.
Are our hearts tonight;
   Put hands on your hearts.
Jesus' love is shining,
   Spread arms up and out.
Showing us the light!

Happy, happy, happy,
   Point to your smiling faces.
Go and spread His love;
   Spread arms apart.
Of this Baby Jesus
   Cradle a baby in your arms.
Sent from God above.
   Point to heaven.

Jesus Was Born

Mary and Joseph were, oh, so tired
Stretch and yawn.
They wanted to go to bed.
Lay head sideways on clasped hands.
There was no room for them at the inn
Shake head from side to side.
So they stayed in the cattle shed.

Jesus was born that very night;
Rock folded arms.
The angels told of His birth.
The shepherds ran to find the Baby,
Run in place.
God's gift to all people on earth.
Spread arms apart.

Jesus is our special friend;
Hug arms across chest.
He forgives the wrongs we have done.
He loves you, and He loves me;
Point to someone; point to self.
Jesus loves everyone!

Tony Moeller

Christmas Tree

This is a tree . . . this is a tree . . .
Close fingers, hands open.
These are the branches
Spread fingers.
And here at the top is the star.
Touch middle finger.
It tells of Jesus, born in a manger
Crook arms.
And Wise Men that come from afar.

Kristin Marsh

Jesus and Simeon

Mary picked up Jesus,
Pretend to pick up baby.
The Savior God had sent;
Point upward.
Wrapped Him in His baby clothes,
Wrap "blanket" around "baby."
Then to the church they went.
Carrying "baby," walk in place.

A kind old man took Jesus.
Extend arms forward, palms up.
He held the Baby small.
Cradle "baby" in arms.
He loved the baby Jesus,
Hug "baby" in arms.
Who came to save us all.
Point to classmates.

Tony Moeller

Baby Jesus Grew

God gave Baby Jesus to the world long ago.
Rock baby in arms.
God took care of Jesus and His family.
Spread arms wide.
Baby Jesus drank milk.
Pretend to drink from cup.
He ate good food.
Pretend to eat with spoon.
Rested,
Lay head to side on folded hands.
And played.
Pretend to play; clap hands.
He grew to be a loving, happy boy.
Stand.

Maybe Jesus helped Mary carry water and grind wheat.
Pretend to carry bucket; rub hands together to grind.
And Jesus helped Joseph pound nails.
Pretend to hammer.
I think He liked to play ball.
Pitch and catch an imaginary ball.

Jesus liked to go to church and hear God's Word.
Walk in place.
He grew to be a man.
Stand tall and reach high.
He went away from home.
Smile and wave.
One day Jesus asked John to baptize Him.
Bend body forward.

Jesus loved people. He made people well.
Stretch out arm and hand.
He gave food to people who needed it.
Make giving action.
Jesus was a loving friend to everyone then. He is my friend now.
Point to yourself.
Jesus always loves ME!
Hug yourself.

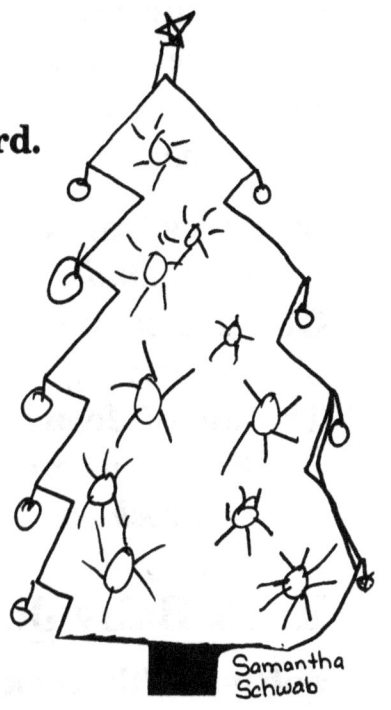
Samantha Schwab

See All the Christmas Trees

**See all the Christmas trees, growing so high;
Pointing like church steeples up to the sky.**

**Hear all the Christmas bells swinging and ringing;
Join all God's children so merrily singing,**

**Singing for Jesus asleep on the hay;
For Christmas, we know is Jesus' birthday.**

The Joy of Jesus' Birth

O God, Your love
Point to heaven.
Goes round and round
Make a circle with your arm.
The people of the earth.
Spread arms wide.

And now I pray,
Fold hands.
Oh, give to me
Point to self.
The joy of Jesus' birth!
*Fold arms over head
and rock on heels.*

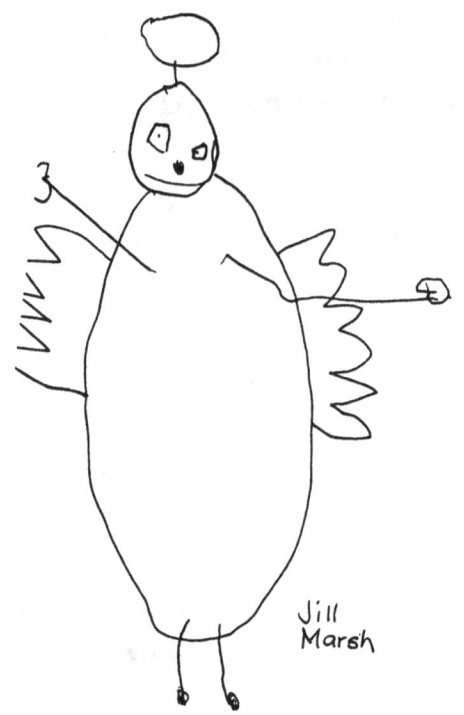

Rock Baby Jesus

Softly, softly rock the Baby;
Rock baby in arms.
Hold Him in your arms.
Hug baby tightly to chest.
Lay Him in His manger bed;
Bend forward and place baby in bed.
Keep Him safe and warm.
Cover baby with blanket.

Tiny little baby Jesus
Point downward at baby in bed.
Came from heaven above;
Point upward.
Came to save us from our sins,
Point to classmates and self.
Gives us God's own love.
Hug self.

"God Made Me" Finger Plays

God Made Me (1)

God made me,
> *Point to self.*

Every part you see:
> *Stretch arms out.*

Ears and eyes and mouth and noses,
> *Point to each.*

Feet with oh so many toes-es
> *Point to feet.*

Skip and jump and hop,
> *Fingers run along, then hop.*

Almost never stop
> *Fingers run again.*

God Made Me (2)

God made me
> *Point to self.*

With eyes to see
> *Point to eyes.*

The whole wide world around.
> *Spread arms.*

God gave me ears
> *Point to ears.*

So I could hear
> *Cup hands behind ears.*

Every lovely sound.
> *Look happy while taking a moment to listen quietly.*

Samantha Schwab

I Have Little Feet

I have little feet
>*Point to feet.*

To follow Jesus' ways.
>*Take a few steps.*

I have little hands
>*Hold hands out.*

And fold them when I pray.
>*Fold hands.*

I have little ears
>*Point to ears.*

That hear of Jesus' love.
>*Cross hands on chest.*

I have a little tongue
>*Point to tongue.*

To tell about His love.
>*Point to classmates.*

Ways to Serve with Smiles

God gave me hands that can do many things.
>*Show hands.*

I can pick up my toys, papers, boxes, and strings.
>*Pick up things from the floor.*

God gave me feet that can walk, skip, and run.
>*Walk, skip, and run in place.*

I can take things to others to help get work done.
>*Carry object and give it to grown-up.*

God gave me a voice that can whisper and sing.
>*Point to mouth.*

I can tell other people: "Jesus is King!"
>*Shout: "Jesus is King!"*

I Have Little Ears

I have little ears
Point to ears.
That hear of Jesus' love;
Cross hands on chest.
I have little lips
Point to lips.
To tell about His love;
Point to classmates.

I have little feet
Point to feet.
To follow Jesus' way;
Take a few steps.
I have little hands
Hold hands out.
To serve Him ev'ry day.
Fling arms wide apart.

Hands on My Head

Play this game, using your hands as follows:

My hands on my head, where I want them to be;
My hands go behind me, where no one can see.

Repeat with "My hands on my shoulders, knees, chin, shoe," etc. Allow the children the opportunity to call out which place their hands are to move to next.

God Gives Me*

(*Invite the children to make up actions to illustrate each line of the verse.)
Eyes so I can see,
Ears so I can hear,
Nose so I can smell,
Teeth so I can chew,
Feet so I can run,
Hands so I can work and play and touch.
God takes care of you and me.
Let's thank Him.

Fun Things to Do

Say, **God made our bodies able to do many things. Let's stretch like a cat;**
—jump like a frog;
—run like a puppy;
—fly like a bird;
—swim like a fish;
—waddle like a duck;
—crawl like a turtle;
—hop like a rabbit;
—sway like an elephant.

"I'm Growing!" Finger Plays

Growing in Jesus' Love

Once I was very, very small.
> *Kneel on floor.*

Sometimes I cried,
> *Rub eyes.*

Sometimes I laughed,
> *Smile or laugh.*

But most of the time I slept.
> *Rest head on hands.*

Whatever I did
Jesus loved me.
> *Point up; then hug self.*

I grew bigger,
> *Begin to stand.*

And bigger,
> *Stand.*

And bigger.
> *Stand tall with hands up.*

Now I can run,
> *Run in place.*

I can jump,
> *Jump in place.*

Or I can stand quietly.
> *Stand in relaxed position.*

Whatever I do,
Jesus loves me.
> *Point up; then hug self.*

Elizabeth Becker

I'm Growing

Now I'm a baby, I look at my toe.
Sit down on floor and look at big toe.
I'm growing, I'm growing! God's helping me grow!
Stand up and raise hands above head.

Now I am two, put my blocks in a row . . .
Pretend to arrange blocks.
I'm growing, I'm growing! God's helping me grow!
Stand up and raise hands above head.

Now I am six, I catch and I throw.
Pretend to catch and throw ball.
I'm growing, I'm growing! God's helping me grow!
Stand up and raise hands above head.

Now I am ten, I shovel the snow.
Pretend to shovel snow.
I'm growing, I'm growing! God's helping me grow!
Stand up and raise hands above head.

Now I'm sixteen, drive a car to the show.
Pretend to drive.
I'm growing, I'm growing! God's helping me grow!
Stand up and raise hands above head.

Now I'm a grown-up. But grown-ups, you know,
Just keep right on growing. God's helping me grow!
Raise hands above head, spin around, then bow.

Every Day I'm Getting Bigger

Jesus worked in many ways
Helping Joseph in his shop.
And His saw went buzz, buzz, buzz,*
As He worked each day.
   (* For additional verses substitute)
     Hammer: pound, pound, pound;
     Plane: swish, swish, swish.

Every day I'm getting bigger
And I can do more things.
I can beat my big bass drum*
Boom, boom, boom, boom, boom.
    **Click the rhythm sticks;*
    Stomp my feet; clap my hands.

Measure Myself

Measure myself, way down to my toes. Sometimes I am tall,
   Stretch body up.
Sometimes I am small,
   Bend down, curl body up.
Sometimes I am very, very tall.
   Stretch body up.
Sometimes I am very, very small.
   Bend down, curl body up.
Sometimes small, sometimes tall,
   Stretch body up, then bend down and curl body up.
See how I am now.

"God's Love" Finger Plays

Sometimes

Sometimes I get very angry
I stamp and scream horribly.
Stamp.
Jesus is sad whenever I'm bad,
Hang and shake head.
But He doesn't stop loving me.
Hug self.

Sometimes I'm really a pouter.
My lip hangs right down to my knee.
Push out lower lip.
Jesus is sad whenever I'm bad.
Hang and shake head.
But He doesn't stop loving me.
Hug self.

Jennifer Boston

Sometimes I'm more of a snatcher.
I grab every toy that I see.
Pretend to grab toy from someone else.
Jesus is sad whenever I'm bad,
Hang and shake head.
But He doesn't stop loving me.
Hug self.

Sometimes when I'm feeling crabby,
I hit my friends hard as can be.
Pretend to hit someone.
Jesus is sad whenever I'm bad,
Hang and shake head.
But He doesn't stop loving me.
Hug self.

Jesus Loves Me All the Time

Dear Jesus, the hands on the clock go round and round.
Move hands.
Sometimes I'm playing.
Pretend to bounce ball.
Sometimes I'm working.
Pretend to sweep with broom.
Sometimes I'm happy.
Smile and jump up and down.
Sometimes I'm sad.
Pretend to wipe tear from eye.
But all the time, Jesus, You're my friend.
Hold clock over head.
You love me all the time.
Hug self.
Thank You, Jesus.

Jesus Loves Me, This I Know

Jesus loves me, this I know.
Point to self.
For the Bible tells me so.
Hold hands together, palms up, like an open book.

Little ones to Him belong.
Stoop down.
They are weak, but He is strong.
Rise and spread arms.

Yes, Jesus loves me.
Nod each of the three times this is sung.
The Bible tells me so.
Hold hands together as above.

Jesus Loves Me Day and Night

Sometimes when I don't do what's right
My friends and I might start to fight.
> *Shake fist.*

But Jesus loves me day and night.
> *Hug self.*

Sometimes when there is no bright light
Then I'm afraid; I'm filled with fright.
> *Cover eyes with hands.*

But Jesus loves me day and night.
> *Hug self.*

Sometimes I'm filled with warm delight
Like when my kite flies out of sight.
> *Point to sky.*

My Jesus loves me day and night.
> *Hug self.*

Sometimes I cry with all my might.
But I know Jesus holds me tight.
> *Pretend to cry.*

Because He loves me day and night.
> *Hug self.*

Clap Your Hands

Clap your hands, shout "Hooray!"
Jesus takes my sins away.
When things go wrong, I stop and pray.
God, I need your love today.

God loves me. God loves you.
God helps me forgive you, too.
Clap your hands. Smile and say,
"God forgives me!" Shout "Hooray!"

Jesus Loves Us When . . .

Jesus
> *Point skyward.*

Loves me
> *Hug yourself.*

When I walk.
> *Walk slowly in place.*

Jesus
> *Point skyward.*

Loves me
> *Hug yourself.*

When I run.
> *Jog in place.*

Jesus
> *Point skyward.*

Loves me
> *Hug yourself.*

When I work
> *Pretend to rake leaves or wash dishes.*

And when I am having fun.
> *Jump up and down on tiptoes and smile.*

Jesus
> *Point skyward.*

Loves you
> *Point at other children.*

When you walk.
> *Walk.*

Jesus
> *Point skyward.*

Loves you
> *Point at others.*

When you run.
> *Jog in place.*

Jesus
>*Point skyward.*

Loves you
>*Point at others.*

When you work
>*Repeat work actions.*

And when you are having fun.
>*Jump up and down on tiptoes and smile.*

Jesus
>*Point skyward.*

Loves us
>*Hug yourself.*

Everyone.
>*Point at each person, then hug yourself.*

God Is Near

Sometimes we're working, picking up toys.
>*Pretend to pick up toys.*

Sometimes we're playing, throwing a ball.
>*Pretend to catch and throw ball.*

Sometimes we're eating.
>*Move hand back and forth from mouth.*

Sometimes we're sleeping.
>*Rest head on hands, palms together.*

Sometimes we're sad.
>*With index fingers, pull down corners of mouth.*

Sometimes we're glad.
>*With index fingers, raise mouth into a smile.*

But all the time
>*Extend arms*

We need not fear
>*Shake head no.*

For our loving God is near.
>*Extend arms upwards and then back down to hug self.*

How Much Does Jesus Love Me?

How much does Jesus love me?
Point to a picture of Jesus.
This much? No!
"Measure" three or so inches with your hands.
That is not enough!
Shake head no.
Jesus loves me so-o-o-o-o-o!
Stretch arms out wide.

How much do I love Jesus?
Point to self.
This much? No!
"Measure" a short distance again.
That is not enough!
Shake head no.
I love Jesus so-o-o-o-o-o!
Arms out wide.

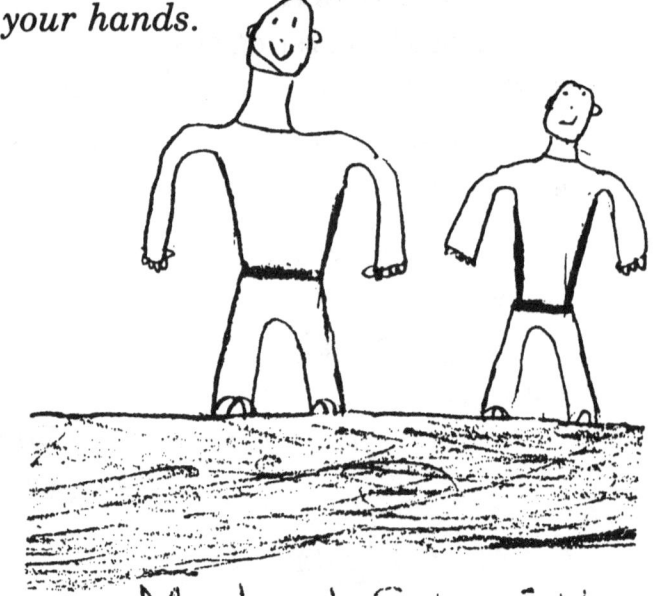

How Many Noses to Smell With?

How many noses to smell with?
Point to nose.
Wiggle it—there is one!
Wiggle nose.

How many eyes go blink, blink, blink
Blink eyes.
When they look up towards the sun?
Look upwards.

How many arms to wave with?
Hold out arms.
Count them—there are two!
Wave one at a time.

How many feet to walk, walk, walk,
Walk in place.
Snug inside each shoe?
Point to each shoe.

How many mouths to talk with?
Point to mouth.
Open it—open it wide.
Open mouth wide.
How many teeth to count, count, count
Touch teeth.
Are hiding there inside?

How many hands to pray with?
Fold hands.

When I Get Tired

When I get tired
Yawn.
And ready for bed,
Rest eyes.
I fold my hands
Fold hands.
And bow my head.
Bow head.
I say my prayers, kiss my mommy,
Pucker and smack.
And turn off the light.
Reach hand up and snap fingers.
Then I pull up the covers,
Pull imaginary covers up to chin.
And I'm ready to sleep.
Lay head on hands.

Sara Freudenburg

This Is Me

This is me.
> *Hold up index finger.*

Here's my friend next door.
> *Hold up middle finger.*

Here's my friend down the street.
> *Hold up ring finger.*

Here are two more.
> *Hold up all fingers of one hand.*

Here are my friends
> *Hold up fingers of other hand.*

Who live far away.
> *Move hand away from the other.*

God loves all people
> *Cross arms on chest.*

In the world today.
> *Make globe with arms.*

Jennifer Booton

Sometimes I Fold My Hands

Sometimes I fold my hands to pray.
Sometimes I lift them high.
Sometimes I kneel.
Sometimes I stand.
Always I know God hears me!

Sometimes I'm happy when I pray;
Sometimes I'm feeling bad.
Sometimes I'm lonely.
Sometimes I'm scared.
Always I know God hears me!

God Will Keep Me Safe

When I'm scared and all alone,
Crouch, wide-eyed.
God will keep me safe.
Stand, hug self.

When I'm far away from home,
Hand shading eyes.
God will keep me safe.
Hug yourself while lying down.

When rain is falling on my head!
Smile, run in place on tiptoes.
God will keep me safe.
Hug self.

Wherever I go, whatever I do,
Arms out to sides.
God will keep me safe.
Hug self.

Because He loves me and He loves you,
Point to self and others.
God will keep us safe.
Give yourself a BIG hug.

"When Jesus Died and Rose Again" Finger Plays

Who Could Take Our Sins Away?

Who could take our sins away?
Extend arms forward, palms up.
Not you, not you, not I.
Point to classmates, then to self.
For our sins we could not pay—
Point to heart, shake head no.
Not you, not you, not I.
Point to classmates, then to self.
Jesus took our sins away—
Point to picture of Jesus or to cross.
Yours and yours and mine.
Point to classmates, then to self.
Thank You, Jesus, thank You!
Fold hands; bow head.

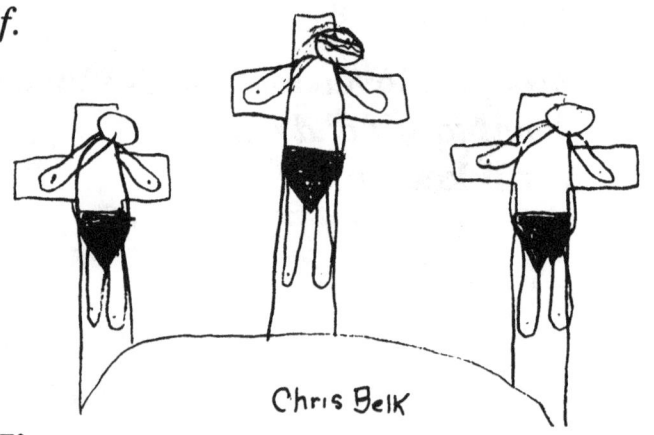
Chris Belk

When Jesus Died

When Jesus died, they buried Him
Crouch down low.
Inside an empty cave.
Make motion outlining "cave."
But Easter came and—happy day—
Make circle with arms to represent sun.
My Jesus is ALIVE!
Again, raise arms above head and jump up.

The Stone Is Gone!

It was a bright and sunny day.
Arms encircle face to make a sun.
Three women slowly made their way
Hold up three fingers.
To Jesus' grave. They planned to go.
Make fingers walk.
He was dead; He suffered so.
Point finger up.
"Who will move the stone aside?"
Raise index finger of other hand; hold both up.
"Oh, look! The stone is gone!" they cried.
Open both hands to hold up open palms.
The angel told them words of cheer.
Point to mouth with both index fingers.
"He is alive. He is not here."
Raise both hands above head.
And so today glad songs we sing
Smile.
To Jesus who lives, our Savior King.

Jesus Is Alive!

Jesus is alive.
Clap, clap.
Jesus is alive.
Clap, clap.
Hooray, Jesus lives!
Clap.
Hooray, hooray, hooray!
Jump up with arms stretched upward on final "hooray."

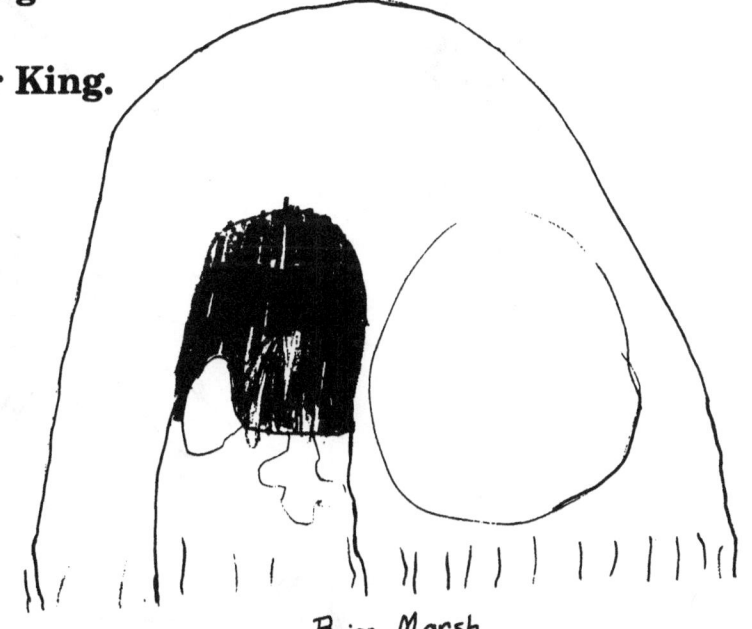
Brian Marsh

We Can Smile

We can smile
> *Smile.*

And clap our hands—
> *Clap once and keep palms together.*

Jesus is alive!

We can sing and pray to Him—
> *With palms still together, bow head.*

Jesus is alive!

He is here
> *Place hand on heart.*

And everywhere—
> *Extend arms.*

Jesus is alive!

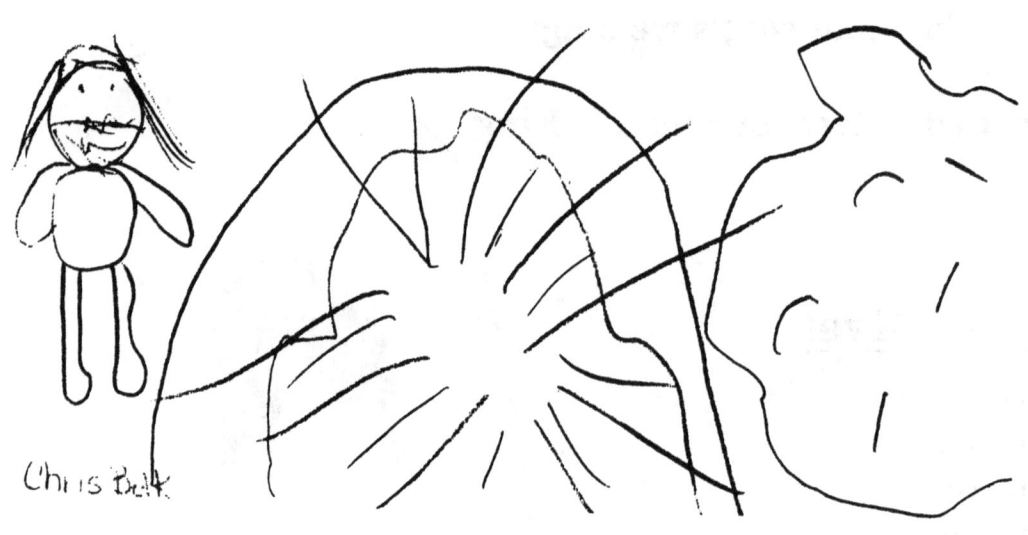

"The World God Made" Finger Plays

All My Blessings

The sun comes up to light the day,
And I can see to work and play.
Thank You for the sun.
> *Point to sun.*

As I walk zigzag down the street,
The leaves go crunch beneath my feet.
Thank You for the leaves.
> *Stamp around.*

I build with blocks; I run my cars.
My teddy helps me watch the stars.
Thank You for my toys.
> *Pretend to build with blocks.*

My friends play games and talk with me,
And sometimes we just watch TV.
Thank You for my friends.
> *Spread hands out, palms up.*

I like to eat; I like to drink,
But peanut butter's best, I think.
Thank You for my food.
> *Pretend to take some peanut butter out of jar and lick lips.*

My grown-ups help me blow my nose,
And get dressed right, and wash my toes.
Thank You for my grown-ups.
> *Hug a grown-up.*

Jesus, You're my friend, I know.
You love me everywhere I go.
Thank You for You.
> *Hug self.*

Most of All

Thank You, God, for everything!
Fold hands in prayer; unfold and open arms at sides.
Thank You for our arms and hands.
Point to each.
Thank You for our eyes and tongues.
Point to each.
Thank You for hamburgers and carrots.
Pat stomach.
Thank You for our homes.
Both arms form peaked roof over head.
Thank You for warm jackets and shirts.
Place both hands on opposite shoulders.
Thank You for families and for our church.
Hold hands with those near.
Thank You most of all for Jesus.
Raise head slowly, look up.
Help us to praise and thank You always.
Open fingers wide, move stiff arms out and up to form V-shape over head.
Amen.
Fold hands and bow heads.

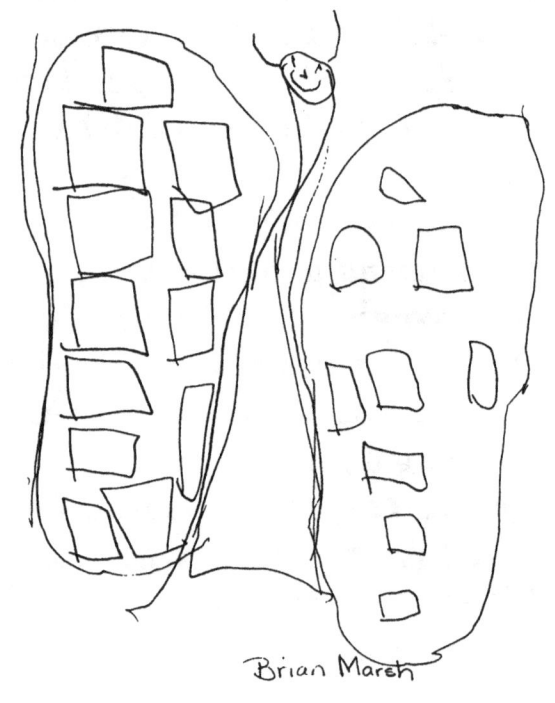
Brian Marsh

Thank You, God, For . . .

Sunshine bright
Point overhead with right hand.
On your arm
Stroke left arm with right hand.
Makes you smile,
Smile happily.
Keeps you warm.
Cross arms over chest.
Thank You, God, for sunshine.

Drink your milk,
> *Tilt head and lift hand in drinking motion.*

Eat your meat,
> *Lift hand to mouth.*

You'll grow big
> *Place palm flat on head and raise it slowly upward.*

When you eat.
Thank You, God, for good food.
> *Lift both arms overhead in prayer and look upward.*

Take a breath—
> *Inhale deeply.*

Hold it tight;
> *Do so.*

Breathe it out
> *Exhale completely.*

Day and night.
Thank You, God, for fresh air.

Close your coat;
> *Move hands past each other near chest.*

Tie your shoe;
> *Revolve hands over shoe top.*

Wear your cap
> *Put cap on head.*

And rubbers, too.
> *Pull on rubbers.*

Thank You, God, for clothes.
> *Lift both arms overhead in prayer and look upward.*

For Little Things

Thank You, God for little things,
For butterflies with pretty wings,
For winds that make the flowers sway,
And other things I've seen today, like—
> *Name things.*

35

The "Me" God Made

God made my head,
Put your hand on your head.
God made my nose,
Put a finger on your nose.
God made my tummy,
Pat your tummy.
And God made my toes.
Point to your toes.
Thank You, God!
Fold hands.

God made my knees,
Put your hands on your knees.
God made my thighs,
Place your hands on your thighs.
God made my shoulders,
Touch your shoulders.
And God made my eyes.
Point to your eyes.
Thank You, God!
Fold hands.

Good Morning, Lord!

Good morning, Lord!
Stand up, stretch arms as high as possible, keep stretching as though you are just waking up.
I'm awake from head to toes.
Touch head and toes five times.
Thank You, Lord, for giving me clothes.
Wiggle into your clothes.
Good morning, Lord!
Stretch to the ceiling.
Thank You, Lord, for toothpaste and comb.
Brush teeth vigorously and comb hair.
Thank You for the warmth of my home.
Rub hands together as if in front of a fireplace.
Good morning, Lord!
Stretch.
Thank You for cereal and eggs.
Pantomime eating.
Thank You for my running legs.
Run in place.
Good morning, Lord!
Stretch.

Kristin Marsh

I love you, Lord.
> *Hands over heart and then point toward sky.*

This is for You.
> *Clapping and cheering.*

Amen! Amen! Amen!

And God Made Me

God made the sun,
> *Hands joined over head.*

God made the trees,
> *Hands separated, swaying above head.*

God made you,
> *Point to someone or to several others.*

And God made me.
> *Point to self.*

God made birds to fly in the sky,
> *Wave arms.*

And fish to swim in the sea.
> *Move arms in swimming motion.*

I'm glad for all the things God made.
> *Smile, move hands apart.*

I'm glad that God made *me*!
> *Smile, point to self.*

Sara Freudenburg

Five Big Apples

Five big apples hanging in a tree,
One fell down just for me.
Four big apples hanging in a tree,
I picked one for you to see.
Three big apples hanging in a tree,
I'll give you one just for free.
Two big apples hanging in a tree,
The wind blew one down, and it landed at my feet.
One big apple smiling down at me,
Thank You, God, for the apple trees.

Chris Belk

We Love You, God!

Thanks, God, for the skies so blue.
Point upward.
Thank You for the good earth, too.
Point down.
Thank You for the tall, strong trees.
Spread arms like branches.
Thank You for the birds and bees.

Thank You for the food we eat.
Rub tummy.
Thanks for flowers, smelling sweet.
Sniff.
Thanks for beds where we can sleep.
Rest cheek on folded hands.
Thanks for legs so we can leap.
Jump.

Thanks for loving us so dear.
Cross hands on chest.
Thanks for sending Jesus here.
Nod.
Thanks for everything You do.
Spread arms, palms up.
Thank You, God! We love You, too!
Hug self.

Thank You, God, I'm Me

**I'm thankful, God, that I can run
And hear the rain and feel the sun.
That I can see a twinkling star,
That I can taste a granola bar!
I'm thankful, God, that I can see.
I'm thankful, God, that I am *me!***

Little Seeds

God makes the sunshine.
> *Hands form a circle overhead.*

God sends the rain.
> *Arms slowly descend, fingers wiggle back and forth.*

The little seeds grow
> *Stoop, hands touching floor.*

Into big plants for food.
> *Slowly stand, raising hands overhead.*

Thank You, God, for food.
> *Fold hands.*

For Friends My Size

Thank You, God, for stars in the sky.
> *Wiggle fingers over head.*

Thank You for birds flying so high.
> *Wave arms as if flying.*

Thank You for legs and ears and eyes.
> *Point to each body part as it is named.*

And thank You for friends just my size.
> *Touch top of head.*

Lightning Bug

Lightning bug, lightning bug, flying in the sky;
> *Open and close both hands, flicking your fingers quickly away from your thumbs.*

Lightning bug, lightning bug, up you go so high.
> *Continue flicking, but raise your hands above your head.*

Lightning bug, lightning bug, tell me, do you know—
> *Stop flicking suddenly and hold your hands wide open, waist high.*

That it is God who makes your magic tail glow?
> *Point up, smile, then hug yourself.*

God Made All Kinds of Food

**God made all kinds of food to grow,
Apples on trees,**
> *Pretend to pick apple.*

Carrots down low.
> *Squat to pick carrot.*

**God's sheep grow wool for my new clothes,
That button tight**
> *Button a coat up the front.*

When the cold wind blows.

**Each night when I climb into bed,
I'll close my eyes**
> *Close eyes.*

And bow my head
> *Bow head.*

**And tell my Father
in heaven above:
"I thank You, God,
for all Your love."**
> *Say this last line together.*

Heather Belk

Clap, Clap, Clap Your Hands

**Clap, clap, clap your hands,
Clap your hands together.
Clap, clap, clap your hands,
Clap your hands together.
Thank You, God for hands.**

Shake, shake, shake your hands, etc.

Nod, nod, nod your head, etc.

> *Add other verses as suggested by teacher or children.*

"My Family" Finger Plays

Daddy and Mom

Who gave us our daddy?
Touch outstretched middle finger.
Who gave us our mom?
Touch outstretched index finger.
Who gave us dear Jesus,
Touch outstretched thumb.
God's very own Son?

**God, our dear Father
In heaven above,**
Point to heaven.
**Gave us these helpers
And gave us His love.**
Cross arms and hug self.

**Thank You, dear Father
In heaven above,**
Fold hands, bow head.
**Help us to obey them
To show You our love.**
Place hand on heart.

Jennifer Boston

The Whole Family

Here is mother so kind and dear,
Here is sister, standing near.
Here is father, tall and straight,
Here is brother, who's almost eight.
Here is baby, sweet but small,
And here's the whole family—
God loves them all.

Many Children

God made many kinds of children, different as can be.
   Hold up ten fingers.
Some are tall and some are small and some are just like me!
   Point to self.
Jesus loves all boys and girls, the little ones quite small,
   Indicate height of small child.
Babies whom you rock to sleep, and children very tall!
   Hands high over head.

"God's Book" Finger Plays

God's Special Book

The Bible is God's special Book,
Cup hands to form an open book.
And He has told us where to look
Point to open "page" on one hand.
To find out all we need to know
Make sweeping circle with arms.
About the love He has to show.
Cross arms on chest.

When I listen and really hear,
Point to ears.
I know that God is always near.
Bring both palms toward shoulders.
And when I look and really see,
Point to eyes.
I know that God loves you and me.
Point to others and then self.

Words about Jesus

Here is my Bible,
Hands together, palms touching.
I will open it wide
Palms open, with little fingers touching.
To read about Jesus from the words inside.
Pretend to read.

"God's House" Finger Plays

A Call to Worship

(Use as an echo pantomime or sing to the tune of "Frère Jacques.")

Teacher: **Come with me.**
    Children: Come with me.
Teacher: **Be my friend.**
    Children: Be my friend.
Teacher: **Come and meet my Jesus.**
    Children: Come and meet my Jesus.
Teacher: **He loves you.**
    Children: He loves me.

Jesus Is There with Me

I like to ride in our car, I do.
I like to ride in our car.
    Make steering motions.
I ride in our car, sometimes quite far.
And Jesus is there with me.
    Point to self.

I like to go to the zoo, I do.
I like to go to the zoo.
    Pretend to be an elephant.
I look at the gnu and the elephants, too.
And Jesus is there with me.
    Point to self.

I like to sail my boat, I do.
I like to sail my boat.
    Pretend to pull boat on a string.

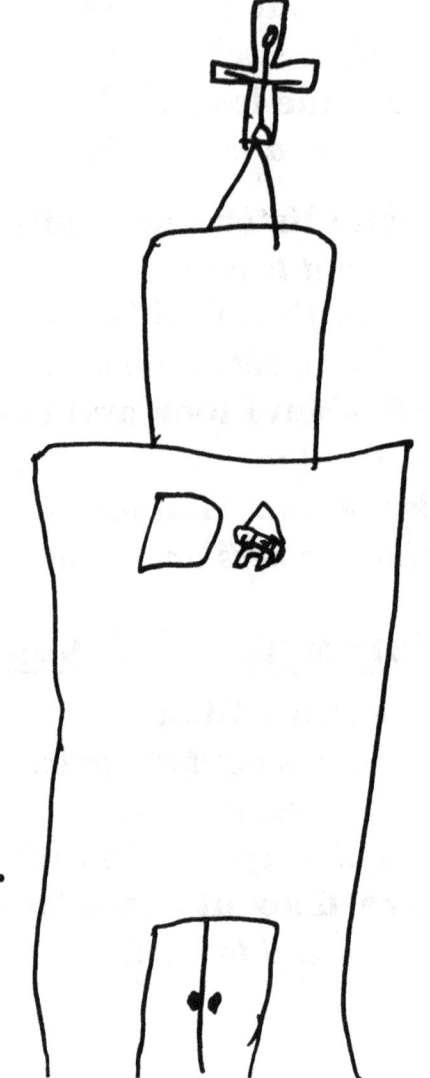

Samantha Schwab

I sail my boat. Boy, can it float!
And Jesus is there with me.
> *Point to self.*

I like to go out and eat, I do.
I like to go out and eat.
> *Rub tummy.*

I eat and I eat till I'm full to my feet.
And Jesus is there with me.
> *Point to self.*

I like to see my friend Paul, I do.
I like to see my friend Paul.
> *Pretend to shake hands.*

I go and see Paul at his house. It's quite tall.
And Jesus is there with me.
> *Point to self.*

I like to stay in my house, I do.
I like to stay in my house.
> *Sit down cross-legged.*

I stay in my house, as snug as a mouse.
And Jesus is there with me.
> *Point to self.*

I go somewhere special on Sunday, I do.
I go somewhere special, I do.
> *Spread arms.*

To church, don't you see? It's nice as can be.
And Jesus is there with me.
> *Point to self.*

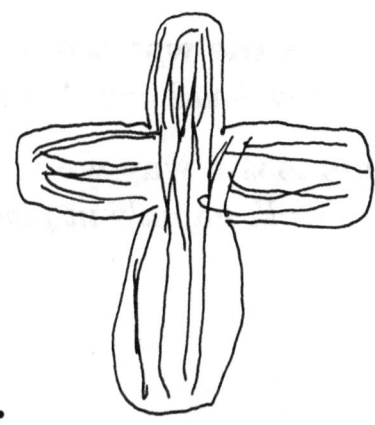

Sara Freudenburg

This Is the Way We Go to Church

(Sing to the tune of "Here We Go 'Round the Mulberry Bush.")

**This is the way we dress for church,
Dress for church, dress for church;
This is the way we dress for church,
Every Sunday morning.**
> *Stretch arms above head as if putting on a sweater.*

This is the way we walk to church, etc.
> *Walk happily in place.*

This is the way we climb the steps, etc.
> *Climb imaginary steps.*

This is the way we sit in church, etc.
> *Sit up straight and attentive.*

This is the way we stand and sing, etc.
> *Stand and pretend to hold a hymnal in front of you.*

This is the way we pray in church, etc.
> *Bow head and fold hands.*

This is the way we leave the church, etc.
> *Walk happily in place.*

"Friends" Finger Plays

God Loves My Friends

Use actions to teach the following words and sing to the tune of "God Loves Me Dearly":

God loves my friends, too,
Point to friends.
Helps me forgive them.
Hug self.
God loves my friends, too,
Point to friends.
As He loves me.
Point to self.
Therefore I'll share His love,
Stretch arms out in front of waist, palms up.
I will forgive them,
Give hugs to friends.
I will forgive them,
Give hugs to friends.
God will help me.
Point up, then to self.

Pray together, asking God to help you each love and forgive one another happily. As you pray, use short phrases. Have the children repeat each phrase after you.

Fun with Friends

Tell the children to do what you say in the motion activity. Change friends each time.

Julia Moskoff

Touch a friend's head.
Touch a friend's toes.
Wiggle a friend's fingers.
Wrinkle your own nose.
Hold hands with a friend and put your hands high in the air.
Twirl yourself around three times beside your own chair.
Stand tall and straight and say, "I'm somebody's friend."
Point to a friend and say, "You're somebody's friend!"
Everyone join hands in a circle and say, "We are God's children today."
"Jesus is *our friend!* Hooray!"

"I Can Help!" Finger Plays

Five Little Helpers

Five little helpers sat down to play.
The first one said, "Have you helped today?"
The second one said, "I have made my bed."
The third one said, "I kissed my Uncle Fred."
The fourth one said, "I buttoned baby's dress."
The fifth one said, "I cleaned up my mess."
Then up jumped the helpers. They shouted, "Hooray!
We like to help others every day."

Jesus Makes Us Kind

Baby crawls;
Paddle with hands.
Down he falls.
Move arms and palms down.
Baby, we will help you.
Lift arms and palms up.
Jesus makes us kind.
Place hand on heart.

People sad?
With index fingers, pull down on corners of mouth.
Make them glad!
With index fingers, raise mouth upwards into a smile.
Play with them and love them.
Cross arms and hug self.
Jesus makes us kind.
Place hand on heart.

Oh, Oh! Mmm! Mmm!

Snip, snip, snip, snip, snip.
Move middle and index fingers in cutting motion.
Sew, sew, sew, sew, sew.
Push "needle" through "cloth"; pick up "clothes."
Go, go, go, go, go.
Walk in place, carrying "clothes."
Tap, tap, tap, tap, tap.
Knock on "door"; hand "clothes" through open "door."
Oh, oh, oh, oh, oh!
Try on "clothes," exclaiming with joy.

Pat, pat, pat, pat, pat.
Knead lump of "dough" in palms of hands.
Bake, bake, bake, bake, bake.
With right hand, take handfuls of "dough" from left hand and insert into "oven."
Take, take, take, take, take.
Take "bread" from "oven" and place into "basket."
Go, go, go, go, go.
Walk in place, carrying "basket" through open "door."
Mmm, mmm, mmm, mmm, mmm!
Eat "bread."

Here Is a Baby

Here is a baby ready for a nap.
Raise index finger.
Put him down into his mother's lap.
Lay finger on other hand.
Cover him up so he won't peep.
Close hand over finger.
Now we'll rock him till he's fast asleep.
Rock hand back and forth.

Old Testament Bible Story Pantomimes

Noah

(An Echo Pantomime)

God said,
    "Noah, Noah.
Build an ark."
    Hammer, hammer.
Gather the animals.
    Come, come.
Close the door!
    Clap, clap.
Down came the rain
    Pitter, patter.
40 days and 40 nights
    Rock, rock.
Out came the sun
    Shine, shine.
Down went the water.
    Dry, dry.
Then Noah came out
    Out, out.
To thank the Lord.
    Praise, praise.
And God said,
    "Never again"
And into the sky He put a rainbow.
    Promise, promise.

Jacob's Dream

Long, long ago in a land far away,
Jacob slept soundly until it was day.
Up overhead in the heavens so high
Twinkled the stars in the quiet night sky.
Jacob was dreaming:
There came a great light,
Angels, a ladder—all shining and bright.
God, our dear Father, was standing there, too,
Promising Jacob, "I'll watch over you."
God makes this promise for us here today:
"I will be with you," He tells us, "always."*

Matthew 28:20

Shhh, Shhh, Don't Let the Baby Cry *(Baby Moses)*

Teacher: **Look at baby Moses.**
    Children: Shhh, shhh, don't let the baby cry.
Teacher: **See how he smiles.**
    Children: Shhh, shhh, don't let the baby cry.
Teacher: **Baby's growing bigger.**
    Children: Shhh, shhh, don't let the baby cry.
Teacher: **What shall we do?**
    Children: Shhh, shhh, don't let the baby cry.
Teacher: **Put him in a basket.**
    Children: Shhh, shhh, don't let the baby cry.
Teacher: **Take him to the river.**
    Children: Shhh, shhh, don't let the baby cry.
Teacher: **Big sister watches.**
    Children: Shhh, shhh, don't let the baby cry.
Teacher: **Princess is coming.**
    Children: Shhh, shhh, don't let the baby cry.
Teacher: **She found the basket.**
    Children: Shhh, shhh, don't let the baby cry.
Teacher: **"What a pretty baby!"**
    Children: Shhh, shhh, don't let the baby cry.
Teacher: **"He shall be my son."**
    Children: Shhh, shhh, don't let the baby cry.
Teacher: **Big sister watches.**
    Children: Shhh, shhh, don't let the baby cry.
Teacher: **"Will you need a nurse?"**
    Children: Shhh, shhh, don't let the baby cry.
Teacher: **"I know a good one."**
    Children: Shhh, shhh, don't let the baby cry.
Teacher: **"Yes," says the princess.**
    Children: Shhh, shhh, don't let the baby cry.
Teacher: **"Bring the nurse to me."**
    Children: Shhh, shhh, don't let the baby cry.
Teacher: **Now the baby's mother**
    Children: Shhh, shhh, don't let the baby cry.
Teacher: **Holds him in her arms.**
    Children: Shhh, shhh, don't let the baby cry.

Teach the children the following phrase, "Shhh, Shhh, don't let the baby cry." Have them whisper it in a shuffling rhythm, making almost a "choo-choo train" sound. Tell the children to put their finger to their lips as they say it. They should repeat the phrase after you say each line in the following story.

David's Song

David watched many sheep.
Shade eyes with hand.
He kept them all quite near.
Hug self.
Sometimes he was afraid.
Shiver with fear.
And sang, "My God is here!"
Confidently shake head yes.
One day King Saul felt bad.
Place hand on forehead.
He yelled and stamped his feet.
Stamp feet.
David took his harp and sang.
Strum harp.
Then Saul fell fast asleep.
Place head on hands.

**"Praise and thanks!
Praise and thanks!"**
Clap hands.
How David loved to sing!
Cup hands over mouth.
**"Praise and thanks!
Praise and thanks!"**
Clap hands.
We let our voices ring.
Cup hands over mouth.

Naaman (1)

Naaman was sick,
Rest head on hands.
Naaman was sad.
Pull corners of mouth down.
God made him well.
Extend forearms, palms up.
Then he was glad.
Pull corners of mouth up.
A little girl helped—
With palm down, indicate own height.
No bigger than you—
With palm down, "measure" classmates.

She told him of God.
Point to heaven.
She said, "He loves you."
Cross arms and hug self.
We can help others.
Point to lips.
We can tell, too.
Point to lips.
Jesus, who loves us,
Cross arms and hug self.
Loves others, too.
Extend arms wide, palms up.

Naaman (2)

Down to the river Naaman went.
   Walk in place.
Seven times he washed.
   Hold up seven fingers.
One, two, three, four, five, six, seven!
   At each count, squat on haunches and rub "water" over arms.
Then he was happy and well.
   Clap hands.

Elijah

The words may be spoken or sung to the tune of "Here We Go 'Round the Mulberry Bush." The four stanzas may be divided among three groups of children, or all four may be played in succession by one or more children. In the former case, have the children representing the brook and the birds (stanzas 1 and 3) start on one end of the room and gradually move to the other end, bringing water and food to the "Elijahs" there (stanzas 2 and 4).

1. **Here we go splashing down the rocks, down the rocks—brook of water.**
   Wiggle fingers and move hands diagonally downward from left to right. Repeat the motions.
2. **Here we go drinking from the brook, from the brook, from the brook; here we go drinking from the brook—thank You, God, for water.**
   Dip "water" from "brook"—i.e., kneeling child on floor—and "drink" from hands. Repeat the motions. Fold hands, bow head for the thank You.
3. **Here we go flying in the sky, in the sky, in the sky; here we go flying in the sky—black birds bringing dinner.**
   Flap arms in rhythm with words.
4. **Here we go eating bread and meat, bread and meat, bread and meat; here we go eating bread and meat—thank You, God, for dinner.**
   Take "food" from "birds"—i.e., child or imaginary birds. Eat food. Fold hands, bow head for the thank You.

King Hezekiah

Dramatize the story by using the following relaxation rhyme:

King Hezekiah was happy one day;
>*Smile happily.*

He went with his friends to the church to pray.
>*Walk in place; then raise hands as if in prayer of praise.*

They prayed together a prayer they knew.

King Hezekiah was sad one day;
>*Look sad; cry.*

He went alone to church to pray.
>*Walk slowly in place; then bow head and fold hands.*

He told God about his troubles.

King Hezekiah was sick one day;
>*Hold one hand on head, another on stomach.*

He stayed lying down in his bed to pray.
>*Close eyes, rest head on hands.*

He asked God to make him well.

King Hezekiah was strong one day;
>*Show arm muscles.*

He laughed and clapped his hands to pray.
>*Laugh and clap hands.*

He thanked God for making him well.

Jonah

Jonah ran away from God—
>*Walk in place.*

Hid inside a ship.
>*Stoop.*

Michael Schmidt

God sent rain. The waves splashed up.
>*Stooping, "twinkle" fingers overhead and then down. Palms up, raise hands.*

The boat went dip, dip, dip.
>*Stooping, rock back and forth.*

Down into the sea he went.
Hands overhead, jump.
In a fish he prayed.
Stooping, fold hands.
Out he flew upon the land.
Jump, then stand erect.
God he now obeyed.
Look up, fold hands.

Jonah walked to Nineveh—
Walk in place.
Preached to everyone.
Extend arms wide.
All the people prayed, and God
Fold hands, bow head. Look up.
Forgave them, everyone.
Extend arms wide.

Daniel

Daniel talked to God each day.
He'd kneel and fold his hands to pray.

The king was tricked by some evil men
To say all people should pray to him.

But Daniel still talked to God above.
He thanked Him for His special love.

The bad men ran to the king to say,
"Daniel prayed to his God today."

Sadly the king punished Daniel then:
He put Daniel in the lion's den!

Daniel asked God for His care.
God sent an angel to be with him there.

The lions' mouths He closed up tight.
God cared for Daniel all through the night.

The king was glad that Daniel was okay.
All the people then prayed to God each day.

New Testament Bible Story Pantomimes

Zechariah and Elizabeth

The time came for Elizabeth to have her baby. It was a boy, just as the angel had said.

Rock imaginary baby.

Everyone was happy because God had been so good to Elizabeth.

Continue rocking.

The day came to name the baby. The people wanted to call him Zechariah, after his father. But Elizabeth said, "No. He's going to be called John."

Shake head and hold out hand in a "stop" gesture.

The people asked Zechariah to tell the name he wanted for the baby, but he still couldn't talk.

Cover mouth with hand.

He asked for a writing tablet and wrote, "His name is John."

Hold imaginary pad and pencil. Write.

Everyone was surprised!

Extend arms in gesture of amazement.

Kristin Marsh

Just then, Zechariah could talk again. He began to praise God!
Extend arms straight, high over head, exuberantly.
The people were amazed. They knew that the baby John was very special.
Nod head slowly in a yes gesture.
Father Zechariah sang a wonderful song.
Strum imaginary guitar slowly.
The Holy Spirit gave him beautiful words to sing about how God had come to His people and was sending His Son, Jesus, as He had promised.
Rock imaginary baby.
Zechariah knew that John would help people get ready for Jesus, their Savior.

Baby Jesus and Anna

Mary and Joseph walked and walked.
Walk in place.
Their donkey walked along, too.
Continue to walk in place.
Clip-clop. Clip-clop. Clip-clop.
Continue walking.
Soon they got to the temple. It was so big.
Shade eyes and slowly look up to the sky, surveying how big the temple is.
They took baby Jesus into the temple.
Pretend to carry a baby.
They thanked God for their baby.
Bow heads and fold hands in prayer.
Anna cried, "Oh, look! The Savior!"
Hold hands, open palms, next to face in surprised look.
"Thank You, God, for baby Jesus!"
Rock baby in your arms and repeat last line once more. Say the words more loudly the last time.

Jesus in the Temple

When Jesus was a little boy,
Extend one arm, palm down, as if measuring a child's height.
His mom and dad were worried.
Palms flat against sides of head.
"Where has He gone?" they asked their friends.
Arms extended in questioning gesture.
Then back to the city they hurried.
Point to distance.
They found Him in the temple-church
Touch fingertips together, forming "roof."
With all the teachers there.
Both hands in front of chest, moving fingers.
"Why did you make us hunt and search?"
Wag index finger in reproach.
Asked Mary with worry and care.
Arms folded across chest.
"I must be in My Father's house."
Fingertips touch to form "roof" again.
His answer then she heard.
"I must be in My Father's house to pray and study His Word."
Hands folded in prayer; then held in front as if an open book.
Then Mary said, "It's time to go."
Beckoning gesture with index finger.
And Jesus made her glad.
Smile, index fingers point on either side of smile.
He knew God wants all boys and girls
Point to head, indicating thinking.
To honor Mom and Dad.
Slightly bow from waist.
Yes, Jesus pleased His parents so that everybody knew
Spread arms expansively.
He had God's love within His heart.
Hands flat over heart.
God's love is in us, too!
Make the sign of the cross.

Jesus Was Baptized

Jesus walked down to the river—
> *Walk toward an imaginary river.*

The Savior God had sent.
> *Point upward.*

John the Baptizer met Him;
> *Children walk in pairs.*

Into the water they went.
> *Pretend to walk into the water.*

John baptized the Savior.
> *One child pretends to pour water on another.*

God's Spirit came down from above.
> *Children move hands down from over heads—fingers are fluttering.*

As Jesus walked out of the water,
> *Children pretend to walk out of the river.*

God said, "See My Son, whom I love."
> *Children cup hands to ears as though listening to God's voice.*

Matthew Levi

Make up pantomime actions to accompany the words of the rhyme below. Use the rhyme to review the facts of Matthew's call. Before you begin, explain to the children that Matthew had another name—Levi. This may be less confusing to them if you ask several children about their middle names by way of explanation.

Matthew Levi sat down in his office one day.
All the people came by with their taxes to pay.
They grumbled and scowled and frowned in disgust.
They said, "Matthew Levi, you're charging too much!"

But Matthew just smiled as he counted his gold.
He thought, "I'll be rich before I am old."
Matthew Levi's big grin didn't last very long—
Deep down in his heart he knew stealing was wrong.

The Lord Jesus walked past Matthew's office one day.
Matthew couldn't believe what he heard Jesus say,
"Follow Me"—just two little words. That was all.
But Matthew obeyed the Lord Jesus' call.

The Savior asked others to follow Him, too.
He forgave all their sins and made them brand new.
"Follow Me"—Jesus still invites us today.
"Jesus, help us to follow You closely," we pray.

The Good Samaritan

A man was walking to Jericho—step, step, step.
Walk in place.
Some robbers jumped out from behind a rock—jump, jump, jump.
Jump three times.
They hit the man
Punching action.
and stole everything he had
Grabbing action.
and then ran away—run, run, run.
Run in place.
The poor hurt man felt very bad—oh, oh, oh.
Hold your head; look dismayed.
Then along came a priest. He worked in the temple-church. Surely he would help!—look, look, look.
Put hand to forehead as if looking into the distance.
He just walked the other way—step, step, step.
Walk in place quickly.
Then came another man. Sure he would stop—look, look, look.
Put hand to forehead once again.
But he, too, just walked the other way—step, step, step.
Step quickly; look afraid.
A third man came, but would he stay? Please, please stay.
Fold hands together as though pleading.
He stopped; he looked; he knelt right down—hooray, hooray, hooray!
Shout it out.
He rubbed on oil, bandaged up the sores, then carried the hurt man away—clip, clip, clop.
Walk in place; lead donkey.

Zacchaeus

Zacchaeus was a little man, as small as he could be.
Stoop down low.
When Jesus came to teach the crowd, Zacchaeus couldn't see.
Make a sad face.
He stood up on his tippytoes and stretched his neck way out.
Stand on tiptoes and stretch neck.
He jumped and jumped to get up high until his tongue hung out.
Jump around, then pant.
At last he cried, "I've got a plan!" And climbed right up a tree.
Pretend to climb a tree.
And from the branches way up high Zacchaeus then could see.
Lean over and look down.
Then Jesus saw him and called out, "Zacchaeus, come down here."
Pretend to climb down tree.
"I'm coming home with you!" Zacchaeus grinned from ear to ear.
Make a happy face.

Jennifer Boston

Jesus and the Children (1)

Jesus taught a crowd one day.
> *Bring outstretched hands together at chest level. Then spread them out, palms up.*

They listened hard to what He'd say.
> *Cup one hand and place it to ear.*

Important teachers came to hear
> *Place hands on chest as though holding lapels.*

While all the people crowded near.
> *Crowd together.*

Suddenly, they heard a noise.
> *Look up as if startled.*

Here came moms and girls and boys!
> *Stretch neck to watch them coming.*

"We came," they said, "to see our friend." But Jesus' men cried, "That's the end!"
> *Throw up hands in disgust.*

"He's too busy. Go away!"
> *Shake index finger as if scolding.*

"Try again some other day."
> *Shoo with both hands.*

Then Jesus cried out, "Wait! Don't go!"
> *Hold right hand above head, index finger up.*

"I love children, too, you know."
> *Point to self and to others in the class.*

"Bring them here for Me to bless."
> *Place right hand gently on children's heads.*

"May God bring you happiness."
> *Repeat these words as you touch each child's head.*

Jesus and the Children (2)

"Let's go to Jesus," some mothers said one day.
Clasp hands and form a circle.
Skip, skip, skip; skip, skip, skip.
Holding hands, skip around circle.
Jesus heard the grown-ups and told the children, "Come."
Hold arms out in invitation, palms up.
"Come, come, come; come, come, come."
Move arms in an inviting motion.
But the friends of Jesus said, "Children, go away."
Facing center of circle, raise right hand in "stop" motion.
"No, no, no; no, no, no."
Shake head in negative motion.
The grown-up people, watching said, "He loves them, everyone."
Cross arms and hug self.
Oh, oh, oh, He loves us, everyone!
Move body left and right in delight.

Sara Freudenburg

Jairus's Daughter

One day the Lord Jesus stood next to the sea.
   Stand tall.
When up came a man as sad as could be.
   Trace "tears" beneath eyes with index fingers.
"Jesus, my little girl's sick and in bed."
   Hold tummy.
"Please come to my house; lay Your hands on her head."
   Hand to head.
While they were walking another man came
   Walk in place.
And said, "I'm so sorry. Oh, what a shame!"
   Shake head.
"Your little girl's dead. Don't walk anymore."
   Sag down.
"The neighbors are crying outside your front door."
   Wipe away tears.
But then Jesus said, "Just believe. Don't be sad."
   Stand tall.
You see, Jesus wanted to make the man glad.
   Smile.
When Jesus walked into Jairus's yard,
   Walk in place.
People were sad; they were all crying hard.
   Sob.
Jesus asked, "What is all this crying, this weeping?"
   Shrug shoulders.
"This girl is not dead. She's only sleeping!"
   Head to shoulder.
Then everyone laughed; but Jesus sent them outside.
   Point with a stern look.
He went and stood by the girl who had died.
   Look down.
Jesus said, "Little girl, get up! Arise!"
   Lift arms up.

Right away she sat up and opened her eyes.
> *Open eyes wide.*

Oh, thank You, Jesus! We love You so much!
> *Clap.*

You brought her to life with only Your touch.
> *Hands out.*

The Blind Man

A blind man sat beside the street.
> *Sit on haunches.*

He heard the Lord one day
> *Tilt head to "listen."*

And felt some mud upon his eyes,
> *Cover eyes with hands.*

Then washed the mud away.
> *"Wash" eyes with hands.*

The blind man then could see the grass.
> *Look at floor.*

He saw the sky so blue.
> *Look upward.*

But best of all, he saw and thanked
> *Fold hands.*

Our Lord, who helps us, too.
> *Point to classmates.*

Jesus Feeds the People (1)

Out in the country up on a hill
Point away and up.
Were many big people and children, all still.
Motion "shhh" on lips.
They listened to Jesus, they listened all day.
Place hand to ear.
They felt very hungry, but no food had they.
Rub stomach; shake head.
"The people must eat," the Lord Jesus said.
Make eating motions.
Then one little boy gave his fish and his bread.
Extend cupped hands in giving.
And Jesus, God's Son, in a wonderful way,
Hands raised in blessing.
Fed all those people and feeds us today.
Fold hands, bow heads.

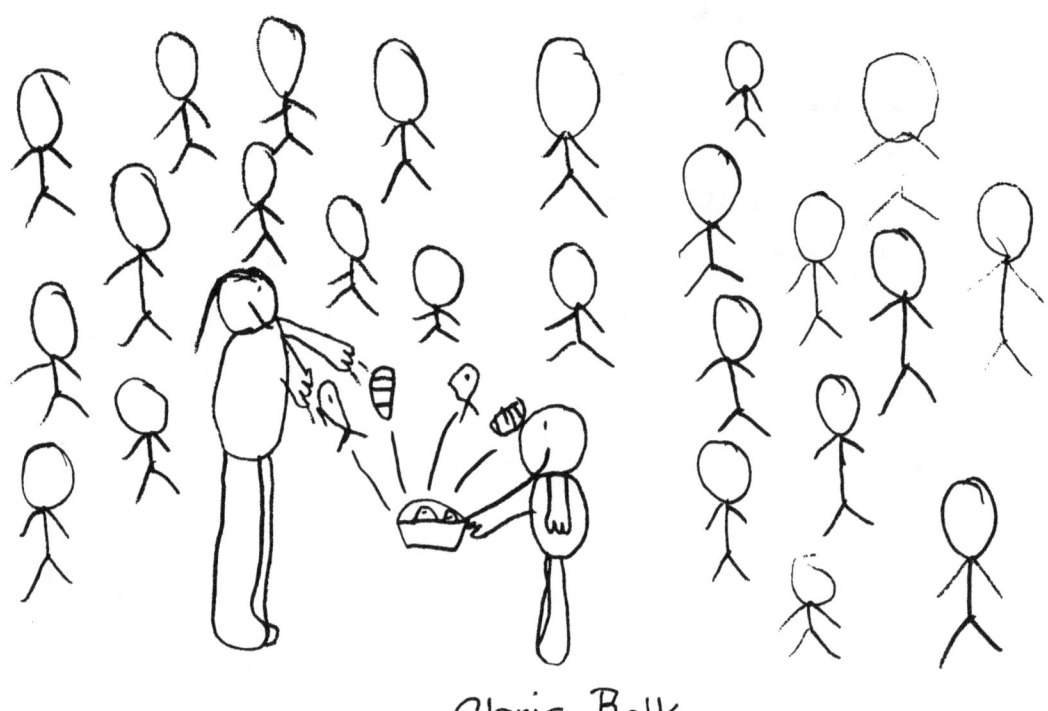

Chris Belk

Jesus Feeds the People (2)

Going for a walk. A long, long walk.
Going to see Jesus! Going to hear Jesus!

Come to a path. A grassy, grassy path.
Can't go over it. Can't go under it. Let's walk down it!

Come to a mountain. A high, high mountain.
Can't go through it. Can't go under it. Guess we'll have to climb it!

Come to a crowd. A huge, huge crowd.
Can't go over it. Can't go under it. Let's sit beside it!

Here comes Jesus! Sweet, sweet Jesus!
See Him heal the sick. Hear Him tell of God. Want to stay here always!

Hear my tummy growling? Loud, loud growling!
No food to eat! Too tired to leave! Look! Jesus gives us food!

Saw Jesus feeding many, many people
See Jesus teaching all about His Father. Isn't Jesus good?

Going for a walk. A long, long walk. A long walk home.
Climb down the mountain. Walk down the path. What a happy day!

Jesus Heals the Lame Man

A man who was lame sat by a gate
Sit on the floor.
At the temple church all day.
Form church frame with hands.
He begged for money,
Hold out hand.
So that he could eat,
Rub stomach.
From those going in to pray.
Fold hands.
Sometimes they gave,
Count "money."
Most times they did not
Shake head and look sadly at empty hands.
As they went through the temple door.
Open "doors."
The man who was lame sat year after year
Point to legs.
And always begged for more.
Hold out hands.
One afternoon as he sat in the sun
Make circle like the sun with both hands.
He looked up and saw two men near.
Stand and walk in place.
There came Peter and John, two of Jesus' good friends,
Smile and hug self.
So the man called out loud and clear.
Cup hands around mouth.
"Give money to me," he begged of the two,
Hold out hand.
"For I haven't eaten all day."
Rub stomach.
Jesus' friends stopped. They said to the man,
Walk in place, then stop.

"We can't give you money today,
> *Count "money" and shake head no.*

But we have something we'll give to you
> *Hold hand out in giving gesture.*

That's worth more than silver or gold.

In Jesus' strong name—stand up and walk,"
> *Smile.*

Peter spoke out the words true and bold.

The man stood right up.
> *Throw hands straight up; spread legs apart.*

He shouted to all, "I can walk! I can run! I can kick!"
> *Click heels in air.*

"What a wonderful thing the Lord Jesus has done!"
> *Smile and spread arms at sides.*

"I tell you, this is no trick!"
> *Shake head; jump up and down.*

Then Peter said, "People, please listen to me."
> *Hold index finger in air as though "preaching."*

"Jesus loves all—it is true."
> *Cross arms on chest; nod assuredly.*

"Come to Him and be saved. He'll fill you with joy."
> *Extend arms outward in inviting motion.*

"Then you will shout praise to God, too!"
> *Raise arms skyward; slowly lower them and fold hands.*

Jesus Prays in the Garden

One night
"Sprinkle" stars in the sky.
Jesus prayed to His Father while His disciples slept.
Close eyes, rest head on hands.
Suddenly
Do a small jump; look startled.
There were lights,
Shield eyes.
And loud noises.
Cover ears.
Jesus' enemies had come.
Look frightened.
Judas walked up to Jesus.
Mark time in place.
He kissed Jesus.
Point to cheek.
Jesus' disciples ran away.
Run in place.
Jesus' enemies tied Him up.
Make winding motion with hand.
And led Him away.
Hold "rope," walk around in small circle.
Jesus stood before Caiaphas, the high priest.
Stand straight and tall.
Caiaphas said, "Are you the Son of God?"
Cup hand behind ear, point with other hand.
Jesus said, "I am."
Nod head.
People slapped Jesus.
Clap hands together once.
They laughed at Him.
Point with finger, make laughing motions.
They were angry at Jesus.
Shake fist.
The soldiers
Stand straight, hold a "spear."

Took Jesus to Pontius Pilate.
Hold "rope," walk in small circle.
Pilate asked Jesus questions.
Cup hand behind ear.
Pilate said, "I can't find anything that Jesus did wrong."
Shake head, hold both hands out, palms out.
The people shouted,
Cup hands around mouth.
"Kill Him! Kill Him!"
Shake fist.
The soldiers
Stand straight, holding a "spear."
Beat Jesus.
Make sharp downward motion with arm.
The soldiers
Stand straight, holding a "spear."
Put a crown of thorns on Jesus' head.
Pat head, make a "hurting" face.
Pilate said, "See the man."
Motion outward with one hand.
The people shouted,
Cup hands to mouth.
"Crucify Him! Crucify Him!"
Shake fist.
Pilate said, "Take Him away."
Make shooing motion with hands.
The soldiers took Jesus away
Hold a "rope," walk in small circle.
To crucify Him.
Hands outstretched.
Jesus did that for me.
Point to self.
Because He loves me so much.
Hug self.
He loves you, too.
Point to other children.
And so do I.
Hug someone nearby.

The Road to Emmaus

Two men were walking;
Two children walk together.
Two men were talking;
The two children pretend to talk.
Two men were sad—as sad as could be.
Heads down; look unhappy.
Jesus was walking;
One child joins the other two.
Jesus was talking;
One child pretends to talk to the others.
"Do not be sad. Be glad! You're with Me!"
All smile.

Cori Freudenburg

Thomas

The following poem can be sung to the tune of "Mary Had a Little Lamb." The words from the second phrase in each line (between the slashes) will be sung three times in the song. Then repeat the first and second phrases together and add the last phrase. Follow this model for all the other stanzas.

Practice the motions before class time. You may wish to record the song on a cassette recorder before class.

Thomas was a / happy man / a joyful man and blest.
Clap in time, stand tall, and smile big.
He was Jesus'/ dear, dear friend / just like all the rest.
Hug self or others.
Jesus died and / rose again, / but Thomas said, "No, no."
Stretch out arms, bring upward to touch fingers over head; then shake head no.
"I won't believe just / go away / and leave me to my woe."
Shake head, make shooing motion with hands, wipe crying eyes.
Jesus spoke to / Thomas once / His love was tall and wide.
Stretch hands up and down, then out to sides.
"Thomas, it is / I, you see, / look at My hands and side."
Point to self, then to palms and side.

"My Lord and God," then / Thomas said, / "You give me faith again."
> *Kneel and hold hand over heart.*

"Now I believe; oh, / thank You, Lord; / I have the joy of 10."
> *Fold hands and smile big as you jump to your feet.*

"Oh, blest are those who / do not see," / said Jesus to them all.
> *Point to eyes and shake head; happy smile on face; motion outward toward others.*

"And yet believe in / Me today. / I will not let them fall."
> *Hold hand over heart, then hug self.*

The Holy Spirit Comes

Jesus said, "My Father in heaven will send the Holy Spirit."
> *Point up.*

"Go to the city. Wait for Him there."
> *Walk in place.*

See all the people watching and waiting;
Praying together in a big, big room.
> *Sit quietly, praying.*

See all the people looking and listening;
No one is walking anywhere.
> *Hold hands to ears.*

Listen! Listen! What can you hear?
Sounds like a big wind coming near.
> *Blow like the wind.*

Look! Look! Over your head!
Little flames of fire—yellow and red.
> *Hold two hands together over head. Wiggle fingers.*

Peter

Chains on his arms,
> *Place forearms together.*

Peter's asleep.
> *Rest head on hands.*

Off fall the chains,
> *Pull forearms apart.*

Up Peter leaps!
> *Stand.*

Puts on his coat,
> *Place arms through "sleeve."*

Shoes on his feet—
> *Place "sandals" on feet.*

Walks past the guards,
> *Tiptoe in place, looking to right and left.*

Runs up the street.
> *Run in place.*

Knocks on a door;
> *Knock on "door."*

Friends let him in.
> *Open "door."*

Oh, they are glad!
> *Throw arms wide in surprise.*

They prayed for him.
> *Fold hands.*

"Thank You, God" Litanies

We Thank You, God

Teacher: **For eyes that can see,**
   Children: We thank You, God.
Teacher: **For ears that can hear,**
   Children: We thank You, God.
Teacher: **For tongues that can taste,**
   Children: We thank You, God.
Teacher: **For noses that can smell,**
   Children: We thank You, God.
Teacher: **For hands that can feel,**
   Children: We thank You, God. Amen.

Thank You, Lord Jesus!

Teacher: **You love us so much!**
   Children: Thank You, Lord Jesus!
Teacher: **You died on a cross for us.**
   Children: Thank You, Lord Jesus!
Teacher: **You took away all our sins.**
   Children: Thank You, Lord Jesus!
Teacher: **Then You became alive again.**
   Children: Thank You, Lord Jesus!
Teacher: **You are our friend forever.**
   Children: Thank You, Lord Jesus!
Teacher: **We love you, Jesus!**
   Children: Thank You, Lord Jesus!
Teacher: **Amen.**
   Children: Thank You, Lord Jesus!

Katie Dedo

Thank You for All Our Gifts

Read each of the following phrases; lead the children in the action indicated and then in the response, "Thank You for all our gifts."

Teacher: **God's Spirit helps some of us write beautiful songs.**
Pretend to write.
Children: Thank You for all our gifts.

Teacher: **God's Spirit helps some of us sing beautiful songs.**
Pretend to sing.
Children: Thank You for all our gifts.

Teacher: **God's Spirit helps some of us build tall buildings.**
Pretend to hammer.
Children: Thank You for all our gifts.

Teacher: **God's Spirit helps some of us sweep the floor clean.**
Pretend to sweep.
Children: Thank You for all our gifts.

Teacher: **God's Spirit helps some of us make sick people well.**
Pretend to listen to heart.
Children: Thank You for all our gifts.

Teacher: **God's Spirit helps some of us make people happy.**
Hug someone.
Children: Thank You for all our gifts.

Thank You, God, for Food

Teacher: **For carrots and turnips and spinach and squash ...**
Children: We praise and thank You, God.

Teacher: **For apples and peaches and bananas and pears ...**
Children: We praise and thank You, God.

Teacher: **For orange juice and milk and cocoa and pop ...**
Children: We praise and thank You, God.

Teacher: **For candy and cupcakes and ice cream and pie ...**
Children: We praise and thank You, God.

Teacher: **For all the good things to eat and drink ...**
Children: We praise and thank You, God.

Thank You, God, for Making Me

God made each of us special. He made us with different parts, each of them special. In our prayer I will name one of the parts. Point to that part with me. Then we will bow our heads, and you will all pray together, "Thank You, God, for making me."

Teacher: **I have two eyes to see with.**
   Children: Thank You, God, for making me.
Teacher: **I have two ears to hear with.**
   Children: Thank You, God, for making me.
Teacher: **I have two hands to clap with.**
   Children: Thank You, God, for making me.
Teacher: **I have two feet to walk with.**
   Children: Thank You, God, for making me.
Teacher: **I have one body to bend with.**
   Children: Thank You, God, for making me.
Teacher: **I have one body to jump with.**
   Children: Thank You, God, for making me.
Teacher: **I have one nose to smell with.**
   Children: Thank You, God, for making me.
Teacher: **I have one mouth to sing with.**
   Children: Thank You, God, for making me.

Jill Marsh

For Sun and Rain and Flowers

Teacher: **For sun and rain and flowers fair—**
   Children: We give thanks, O God, we give thanks.
Teacher: **For house and food and clothes to wear—**
   Children: We give thanks, O God, we give thanks.
Teacher: **For eyes and ears and feet that run—**
   Children: We give thanks, O God, we give thanks.
Teacher: **But most of all, for Your dear Son—**
   Children: We give thanks, O God, we give thanks.

Thank You, God, for Homes

Teacher: **For turtle homes,**
 Children: Thank You, God.
Teacher: **For homes for dogs,**
 Children: Thank You, God.
Teacher: **For apartment homes,**
 Children: Thank You, God.
Teacher: **For houseboat homes,**
 Children: Thank You, God.
Teacher: **For trailer homes,**
 Children: Thank You, God.
Teacher: **For houses,**
 Children: Thank You, God.
Teacher: **For churches,**
 Children: Thank You, God.
Teacher: **For sending Jesus so that someday we can live forever with You,**
 Children: Thank You, God.

"Help Us, God" Litanies

Help Us Be Good Helpers

The children are to act out each of the helpers you mention and then respond with "Help us be good helpers, too."

Teacher: **Thank You, God, for police helpers.**
Pretend to direct traffic.
Children: Help us be good helpers, too.
Teacher: **Thank You, God, for firefighter helpers.**
Pretend to squirt hose at fire.
Children: Help us be good helpers, too.
Teacher: **Thank You, God, for grocery store helpers.**
Pretend to ring cash register.
Children: Help us be good helpers, too.
Teacher: **Thank You, God, for farmer helpers.**
Pretend to dig in ground.
Children: Help us be good helpers, too.
Teacher: **Thank You, God, for teacher helpers.**
Pretend to write on chalkboard.
Children: Help us be good helpers, too.
Teacher: **Thank You, God, for our best Helper, Jesus.**
Hug self.
Children: Help us be good helpers, too.

Jesus Our Good Friend

Teacher: **Jesus, You were a good friend to Peter.**
    Children: Help me to be a good friend, too.
Teacher: **You were a good friend to sick people and made them well.**
    Children: Help me to be a good friend, too.
Teacher: **You were a good friend to sad people and made them happy.**
    Children: Help me to be a good friend, too.
Teacher: **You understood people and forgave them when they did naughty things.**
    Children: Help me to be a good friend, too.
Teacher: **You were a good friend to children.**
    Children: Help me to be a good friend, too.
Teacher: **Jesus, You are still a good friend to me and everybody.**
    Children: Help me to be a good friend, too.

We Are God's Special Children

Teacher: **We all are Your special children, God.**
    Children: Help us to love one another.
Teacher: **Sometimes we forget this, God.**
    Children: Help us to love one another.
Teacher: **Sometimes we fight each other, God.**
    Children: Help us to love one another.
Teacher: **Sometimes we make each other cry.**
    Children: Help us to love one another.
Teacher: **You sent us Jesus to be our friend.**
    Children: Help us to love one another.
Teacher: **Jesus loves us very much.**
    Children: Help us to love one another.
Teacher: **Help us to be like Jesus.**
    Children: Help us to love one another.

Feelings

Teacher: **Sometimes we feel sad.**
   Pretend to cry.
  Children: But God will always help us.
Teacher: **Sometimes we feel scared.**
  Knock knees, chatter teeth, and cry "OOOOO!"
  Children: But God will always help us.
Teacher: **Sometimes we feel lonely.**
  Lip should quiver.
  Children: But God will always help us.
Teacher: **We may feel many different things.**
  Children: But God will always help us.

Children Can Do Important Things

Teacher: **Children can do important things.**
  Children: Help us, Holy Spirit.
Teacher: **Children can make God's world a happier place.**
  Children: Help us, Holy Spirit.
Teacher: **Children can tell people about Jesus.**
  Children: Help us, Holy Spirit.
Teacher: **Children can make things and sing songs.**
  Children: Help us, Holy Spirit.
Teacher: **Children can do loving things.**
  Children: Help us, Holy Spirit.

We Are God's Children

Teacher: **In the morning we're happy to say,**
  Children: We are God's children!
Teacher: **God will be with us all through the day.**
  Children: We are God's children!
Teacher: **He gives us food, clothing, and friends.**
  Children: We are God's children!
Teacher: **His love for us will never end.**
  Children: We are God's children!

Jesus Is Stronger

Teacher: **Bulldozers are strong and push dirt around, but . . .**
    Children: Jesus is stronger than everything.
Teacher: **Elephants can pull up trees with their trunks, but . . .**
    Children: Jesus is stronger than everything.
Teacher: **Planes can fly fast and far in the sky, but . . .**
    Children: Jesus is stronger than everything.
Teacher: **Cars can go fast and make lots of noise, but . . .**
    Children: Jesus is stronger than everything.
Teacher: **Eagles are strong and beautiful and brave, but . . .**
    Children: Jesus is stronger than everything.
Teacher: **Hospitals are a good place to get well, but . . .**
    Children: Jesus is stronger than everything.

God Cares about You

Teacher: **When you wake up,**
    Children: God cares about you.
Teacher: **When you brush your teeth,**
    Children: God cares about you.
Teacher: **When you get dressed,**
    Children: God cares about you.
Teacher: **When you play with your friends outside,**
    Children: God cares about you.
Teacher: **When you eat your lunch,**
    Children: God cares about you.
Teacher: **When you swing in the park,**
    Children: God cares about you.
Teacher: **When you fall off your bike,**
    Children: God cares about you.
Teacher: **When you hop into bed at night,**
    Children: God cares about you.
Teacher: **When you are sleeping,**
    Children: God cares about you.

"I'm Sorry" Litanies

Jesus, I Am Sorry

Teacher: **Sometimes I say unkind words to my family or friends.**
  Children: Jesus, I am sorry. Please forgive me.
Teacher: **Sometimes I fight with my family or friends and hit them.**
  Children: Jesus, I am sorry. Please forgive me.
Teacher: **Sometimes I forget to tell my friends about my best friend, Jesus.**
  Children: Jesus, I am sorry. Please forgive me.
Teacher: **Sometimes I don't obey my parents.**
  Children: Jesus, I am sorry. Please forgive me.
Teacher: **Sometimes I don't listen or worship in church.**
  Children: Jesus, I am sorry. Please forgive me.
Teacher: **Sometimes I take things that don't belong to me.**
  Children: Jesus, I am sorry. Please forgive me.

God Is Full of Love

Teacher: **God is full of love; He loves us even when we are bad.**
  Children: Create in me a clean heart, O God.
Teacher: **When we ask in Jesus' name, God forgives us.**
  Children: Create in me a clean heart, O God.
Teacher: **God forgives; He doesn't punish us as we deserve.**
  Children: Create in me a clean heart, O God.
Teacher: **His love for us is as big as the sky above.**
  Children: Create in me a clean heart, O God.
Teacher: **He takes our sins away and gives us a new start.**
  Children: Create in me a clean heart, O God.
Teacher: **He is our heavenly Father; He takes care of us.**
  Children: Create in me a clean heart, O God.

"All about Jesus" Litanies

I've Got a Friend

Teacher: **Even when my other friends go away,**
    Children: I've got a friend!
Teacher: **Even when my pets don't want to play with me,**
    Children: I've got a friend!
Teacher: **Even when my grown-ups are too busy to play with me,**
    Children: I've got a friend!
Teacher: **Even when I'm all by myself,**
    Children: I've got a friend!
Teacher: **Jesus is my friend, so I can say all the time,**
    Children: "I've got a friend!"

Lord, Teach Us to Pray

Teacher: **When we are happy,**
    Children: Lord, teach us to pray.
Teacher: **When we are sad,**
    Children: Lord, teach us to pray.
Teacher: **When we are busy,**
    Children: Lord, teach us to pray.
Teacher: **When we are resting,**
    Children: Lord, teach us to pray.
Teacher: **When we are eating,**
    Children: Lord, teach us to pray.
Teacher: **When we are hurting,**
    Children: Lord, teach us to pray.
Teacher: **When we are giggling,**
    Children: Lord, teach us to pray.
Teacher: **Every day,**
    Children: Lord, teach us to pray.

Alison Atwood

Jesus Promised to Be with Me

Teacher: **When I'm sick and feel awful, and my friends can't come see me,**
    Children: Jesus promised to be with me.
Teacher: **When I'm scared and alone,**
    Children: Jesus promised to be with me.
Teacher: **When people do things that are mean to me,**
    Children: Jesus promised to be with me.
Teacher: **When I do bad things, and everyone gets mad,**
    Children: Jesus promised to be with me.
Teacher: **When good things are happening, and I'm feeling glad,**
    Children: Jesus promised to be with me.
Teacher: **All the time, any time, no matter what happens,**
    Children: Jesus promised to be with me.

Cori Freudenburg

Jesus Is Born! Let's Shout for Joy!

Teacher: **People waited and waited, and then He came!**
    Children: Jesus is born! Let's shout for joy.
Teacher: **He came to a stable so small and poor.**
    Children: Jesus is born! Let's shout for joy.
Teacher: **The angels sang the glad good news.**
    Children: Jesus is born! Let's shout for joy.
Teacher: **The shepherds heard and ran to see.**
    Children: Jesus is born! Let's shout for joy.
Teacher: **And now let's tell the whole wide world:**
    Children: Jesus is born! Let's shout for joy.

On Christmas Day

Lead the children in this action, responsive litany:

Teacher: **Then all the bells on earth shall ring.**
With palms together, swing your arms to and fro in front of your body.
Children: On Christmas Day, on Christmas Day.
Imitate the previous motion of the teacher.

Teacher: **And all the bells on earth shall ring.**
Repeat the above motion.
Children: On Christmas Day, on Christmas Day.
Repeat the above motion.

Teacher: **And all the angels in heaven shall sing.**
Look up and move hand in wide arc above head.
Children: On Christmas Day, on Christmas Day.
Repeat teacher's motion.

Teacher: **And all the angels in heaven shall sing.**
Repeat above motion.
Children: On Christmas Day, on Christmas Day.
Repeat teacher's motion.

Teacher: **And all the people on earth shall sing.**
Look at and include the whole group with a slow sweep of the hand.
Children: On Christmas Day, on Christmas Day.
Imitate teacher's motion.

Teacher: **And all the people on earth shall sing.**
Repeat same motion.
Children: On Christmas Day, on Christmas Day.
Repeat teacher's motion.

Kristin Marsh

"Praise God" Litanies

Praise the Lord

Teacher: **We come to worship and praise our God. Let us begin in the name of the Father, and of the Son, and of the Holy Spirit. Amen.**
    Children: Praise the Lord!
Teacher: **Praise God in His church.**
    Children: Praise the Lord!
Teacher: **Praise God in our classroom.**
    Children: Praise the Lord!
Teacher: **Praise Him outside on the playground.**
    Children: Praise the Lord!
Teacher: **Praise Him for all the things He has done.**
    Children: Praise the Lord!
Teacher: **Praise Him for lunch and recess.**
    Children: Praise the Lord!
Teacher: **Praise Him with music.**
    Children: Praise the Lord!
Teacher: **Praise Him with joyful dancing.**
    Children: Praise the Lord!
Teacher: **Praise Him with guitar and piano.**
    Children: Praise the Lord!
Teacher: **Praise Him with rhythm instruments.**
    Children: Praise the Lord!
Teacher: **Let the whole world**
    Children: Praise the Lord!

Alleluia, Alleluia

Teacher: **In spring the grass has new life.**
    Children: Alleluia, alleluia.
Teacher: **In spring the trees have new life.**
    Children: Alleluia, alleluia.
Teacher: **Jesus, You rose from the dead and have new life.**
    Children: Alleluia, alleluia.
Teacher: **Jesus, You rose and gave us new life.**
    Children: Alleluia, alleluia.

Sara Freudenburg

We're Going to Heaven

Teacher: **Jesus lives!**
    Children: We're going to heaven.
Teacher: **Because He lives,**
    Children: We're going to heaven.
Teacher: **We're not afraid of death.**
    Children: We're going to heaven.
Teacher: **Jesus is stronger than death.**
    Children: We're going to heaven.
Teacher: **Jesus promised us**
    Children: We're going to heaven.
Teacher: **We believe in Jesus.**
    Children: We're going to heaven.

Heaven Is My Home

Teacher: **I was born here on earth, but**
    Children: Heaven is my home.
Teacher: **I have a family and friends here, but**
    Children: Heaven is my home.
Teacher: **God made a beautiful world for me, but**
    Children: Heaven is my home.
Teacher: **God made birds to fly and sing, flowers and grass to grow, animals that run and hop and jump, but**
    Children: Heaven is my home.
Teacher: **Sin ruined God's beautiful world. Things are sometimes ugly and dirty and scary here, but**
    Children: Heaven is my home.
Teacher: **Jesus died on the cross so that my sins are forgiven.**
    Children: Heaven is my home.
Teacher: **He rose again from the dead on Easter and went back to heaven to prepare a place for me, so**
    Children: Heaven is my home.
Teacher: **Jesus is coming again to take me to live with Him in His beautiful home.**
    Children: Heaven is my home.
Teacher: **There will be no crying or hurting, only singing and laughing, loving and praising God. Best of all, Jesus will be there.**
    Children: Heaven is my home.
Teacher: **Jesus will take me to heaven someday. Thank You, Jesus, thank You.**
    Children: Heaven is my home.
Teacher: **Amen.**

Contributors

Beverly Beckmann, Donna Bobb, Susan Brandt, Mary L. Brummer, Nancy Carlson, Annetta Dellinger, Joanne Eisenberg, Jane L. Fryar, Elizabeth Friedrich, Earl Gaulke, Carol Greene, Jane Haas, Martha Streufert Jander, Julaine Kammrath, Robert Kerman, Lorna Menzel, Shirley K. Morgenthaler, Gayle Timken, Michale Tremblay, Debbie Stroh, Judy Williams, Nancy Warner.

Topical Index

Finger Plays

"Baby Jesus Is Born!" Finger Plays — 7
    Baby Jesus Grew — 12
    Christmas Tree — 11
    Come, Lord Jesus! — 9
    Happy, Happy, Happy — 10
    Jesus and Simeon — 12
    Jesus Was Born — 11
    Mary and the Angel — 7
    One Night in Bethlehem — 8
    Rock Baby Jesus — 14
    See All the Christmas Trees — 13
    The Best Present of All — 8
    The Joy of Jesus' Birth — 14
    Walk to the Manger — 10
    Wise Men — 9

"God Made Me" Finger Plays — 15
    Fun Things to Do — 17
    God Gives Me — 17
    God Made Me (1) — 15
    God Made Me (2) — 15
    I Have Little Ears — 17
    I Have Little Feet — 16
    My Hands on My Head — 17
    Ways to Serve with Smiles — 16

"I'm Growing" Finger Plays — 18
    Everyday I'm Getting Bigger — 20
    Growing in Jesus' Love — 18
    I'm Growing — 19
    Measure Myself — 20

"God's Love" Finger Plays — 21
    Clap Your Hands — 23
    God Is Near — 25
    God Will Keep Me Safe — 29
    How Many Noses to Smell With? — 26
    How Much Does Jesus Love Me? — 26
    Jesus Loves Me All the Time — 22
    Jesus Loves Me Day and Night — 23
    Jesus Loves Me, This I Know — 22
    Jesus Loves Us When . . . — 24
    Sometimes — 21
    Sometimes I Fold My Hands — 28
    This Is Me — 28
    When I Get Tired — 27

"When Jesus Died and Rose Again" Finger Plays — 30
    Jesus Is Alive! — 31
    The Stone Is Gone! — 31
    We Can Smile — 32
    When Jesus Died — 30
    Who Could Take Our Sins Away? — 30

"The World God Made" Finger Plays — 33
    All My Blessings — 33
    And God Made Me — 37
    Clap, Clap, Clap Your Hands — 40
    Five Big Apples — 37
    For Friends My Size — 39
    For Little Things — 35
    Good Morning, Lord! — 36
    God Made All Kinds of Food — 40
    Lightning Bug — 39
    Little Seeds — 39
    Most of All — 34
    Thank You, God, For . . . — 34
    Thank You, God, I'm Me — 38
    The "Me" God Made — 36
    We Love You, God! — 38

"My Family" Finger Plays — 41
    Daddy and Mom — 41
    Many Children — 42
    The Whole Family — 42

"God's Book" Finger Plays — 43
    God's Special Book — 43
    Words about Jesus — 43

"God's House" Finger Plays — 44
    A Call to Worship — 44
    Jesus Is There with Me — 44
    This Is the Way We Go to Church — 46

"Friends" Finger Plays — 47
    Fun with Friends — 47
    God Loves My Friends — 47

"I Can Help" Finger Plays — 48
    Five Little Helpers — 48
    Here Is a Baby — 49
    Jesus Makes Us Kind — 48
    Oh, Oh! Mmm! Mmm! — 49

Bible Story Pantomimes

Old Testament — 50
- Daniel — 55
- David's Song — 52
- Elijah — 53
- Jacob's Dream — 50
- Jonah — 54
- King Hezekiah — 54
- Naaman (1) — 52
- Naaman (2) — 53
- Noah — 50
- Shhh, Shhh, Don't Let the Baby Cry — 51

New Testament — 56
- Baby Jesus and Anna — 57
- Jairus's Daughter — 64
- Jesus and the Children (1) — 62
- Jesus and the Children (2) — 63
- Jesus Feeds the People (1) — 66
- Jesus Feeds the People (2) — 67
- Jesus Heals the Lame Man — 68
- Jesus in the Temple — 58
- Jesus Prays in the Garden — 70
- Jesus Was Baptized — 59
- Matthew Levi — 59
- Peter — 74
- The Blind Man — 65
- The Good Samaritan — 60
- The Holy Spirit Comes — 73
- The Road to Emmaus — 72
- Thomas — 72
- Zacchaeus — 61
- Zechariah and Elizabeth — 56

Litanies

"Thank You, God" Litanies — 75
- For Sun and Rain and Flowers — 77
- Thank You for All Our Gifts — 76
- Thank You, God, for Food — 76
- Thank You, God, for Homes — 78
- Thank You, God, for Making Me — 77
- Thank You, Lord Jesus! — 75
- We Thank You, God — 75

"Help Us, God" Litanies — 79
- Children Can Do Important Things — 81
- Feelings — 81
- God Cares about You — 82
- Help Us Be Good Helpers — 79
- Jesus Is Stronger — 82
- Jesus Our Good Friend — 80
- We Are God's Children — 81
- We Are God's Special Children — 80

"I'm Sorry" Litanies — 83
- God Is Full of Love — 83
- Jesus, I Am Sorry — 83

"All about Jesus" Litanies — 84
- I've Got a Friend — 84
- Jesus Is Born! Let's Shout for Joy! — 85
- Jesus Promised to Be with Me — 85
- Lord, Teach Us to Pray — 84
- On Christmas Day — 86

"Praise God" Litanies — 87
- Alleluia, Alleluia — 88
- Heaven Is My Home — 89
- Praise the Lord — 87
- We're Going to Heaven — 88

Index of Titles

Finger Plays and Litanies

A Call to Worship	44
Alleluia, Alleluia	88
All My Blessings	33
And God Made Me	37
Baby Jesus Grew	12
Children Can Do Important Things	81
Christmas Tree	11
Clap Your Hands	23
Clap, Clap, Clap Your Hands	40
Come, Lord Jesus!	9
Daddy and Mom	41
Everyday I'm Getting Bigger	20
Feelings	81
Five Big Apples	37
Five Little Helpers	48
For Friends My Size	39
For Little Things	35
For Sun and Rain and Flowers	77
Fun Things to Do	17
Fun with Friends	47
God Cares about You	82
God Gives Me	17
God Is Full of Love	83
God Is Near	25
God Loves My Friends	47
God Made All Kinds of Food	40
God Made Me (1)	15
God Made Me (2)	15
God's Special Book	43
God Will Keep Me Safe	29
Good Morning, Lord!	36
Growing in Jesus' Love	18
Hands on my Head	17
Happy, Happy, Happy	10
Heaven Is My Home	89
Help Us Be Good Helpers	79
Here Is a Baby	49
How Many Noses to Smell With?	26
How Much Does Jesus Love Me?	26
I Have Little Ears	17
I Have Little Feet	16
I'm Growing	19
I've Got a Friend	84
Jesus and Simeon	12
Jesus, I Am Sorry	83
Jesus Is Alive!	31
Jesus Is Born! Let's Shout for Joy!	85
Jesus Is Stronger	82
Jesus Is There with Me	44
Jesus Loves Me All the Time	22
Jesus Loves Me Day and Night	23
Jesus Loves Me, This I Know	22
Jesus Loves Us When . . .	24
Jesus Makes Us Kind	48
Jesus Our Good Friend	80
Jesus Promised to Be with Me	85
Jesus Was Born	11
Lightning Bug	39
Little Seeds	39
Lord, Teach Us To Pray	84
Many Children	42
Mary and the Angel	7
Measure Myself	20
Most of All	34
My Hands on My Head	17
Oh, Oh! Mmm! Mmm!	49
On Christmas Day	86
One Night in Bethlehem	8
Praise the Lord	87
Rock Baby Jesus	14
See All the Christmas Trees	13
Sometimes	21
Sometimes I Fold My Hands	28
Thank You for All Our Gifts	76
Thank You, God, For . . .	34
Thank You, God, for Food	76
Thank You, God, for Homes	78
Thank You, God, for Making Me	77
Thank You, God, I'm Me	38
Thank You, Lord Jesus!	75
The Best Present of All	8

The Joy of Jesus' Birth	14	Jacob's Dream	50
The "Me" God Made	36	Jairus's Daughter	64
The Stone Is Gone!	31	Jesus and the Children (1)	62
The Whole Family	42	Jesus and the Children (2)	63
This Is Me	28	Jesus Feeds the People (1)	66
This Is The Way We Go to Church	46	Jesus Feeds the People (2)	67
		Jesus Heals the Lame Man	68
Walk to the Manger	10	Jesus in the Temple	58
Ways to Serve with Smiles	16	Jesus Prays in the Garden	70
We Are God's Children	81	Jesus Was Baptized	59
We Are God's Special Children	80	Jonah	54
We Can Smile	32		
We Love You, God!	38	King Hezekiah	54
We Thank You, God	75		
We're Going to Heaven	88	Matthew Levi	59
When I Get Tired	27		
When Jesus Died	30	Naaman (1)	52
Who Could Take Our Sins Away?	30	Naaman (2)	53
Wise Men	9	Noah	50
Words about Jesus	43		
		Peter	74

Bible Story Pantomimes

Baby Jesus and Anna	57	Shhh, Shhh, Don't Let the Baby Cry	51
Daniel	55	The Blind Man	65
David's Song	52	The Good Samaritan	60
		The Holy Spirit Comes	73
Elijah	53	The Road to Emmaus	72
		Thomas	72
		Zacchaeus	61
		Zechariah and Elizabeth	56

Songs of God's Love
A Hymnal for Primary Children

It makes music easy for you and your students!

Songs of God's Love helps you introduce the joys of singing to your primary students. This collection of 100 songs is the result of three years of research, collecting, and editing—work that's produced these helpful features for both you and your students...

- easy-to-play piano accompaniments, plus chords for guitar or autoharp
- words for all songs printed separately—so youngsters can follow along
- settings pitched for a young child's voice
- songs indexed by title *and* first lines
- songs grouped by seasons of church year, special events, holidays

Songs of God's Love is also available in a convenient audiocassette package. This package contains all 100 songs on four audiocassette tapes, a User's Guide, and one copy of the **Songs of God's Love** hymnal—all packaged in an attractive vinyl case for safe storage.

Use **Songs of God's Love** to enhance Sunday School, dayschool, VBS, or playtime at home—wherever you share music with primary-age children!

To order, contact your Christian bookstore or call TOLL FREE

CONCORDIA PUBLISHING HOUSE

1-800-325-3040

Hymnal 03GAA1150 $7.95
Audiocassette package 79GAA9980 $34.95

© 1989 Concordia

www.ingramcontent.com/pod-product-compliance
Lightning Source LLC
Chambersburg PA
CBHW080348170426
43194CB00014B/2723